CITY IN THE SUN

THE JAPANESE CONCENTRATION CAMP AT POSTON, ARIZONA

BOOKS BY PAUL BAILEY

Fiction

> FOR TIME AND ALL ETERNITY
> FOR THIS MY GLORY
> TYPE HIGH
> THE GAY SAINT
> SONG EVERLASTING
> THE CLAWS OF THE HAWK
> GHOST DANCE MESSIAH

Mystery Fiction

> DELIVER ME FROM EVA

History and Biography

> THE ARMIES OF GOD (The Little Known Story of the Mormon Militia on the American Frontier)
> SAM BRANNAN AND THE CALIFORNIA MORMONS
> FABULOUS FARMER (the Story of Walter Knott and His Berry Farm)—with Roger Holmes.
> WALKARA, HAWK OF THE MOUNTAINS
> WOVOKA, THE INDIAN MESSIAH
> GRANDPA WAS A POLYGAMIST
> JACOB HAMBLIN, BUCKSKIN APOSTLE
> CITY IN THE SUN

Editor and Compiler of

> THE MORMONS IN CALIFORNIA
> (Pioneer Journal of William Glover)

THE JAPANESE CONCENTRATION CAMP
AT POSTON, ARIZONA

CITY IN THE SUN

by

PAUL BAILEY

WESTERNLORE PRESS . . . 1971 . . . LOS ANGELES 90041

Published Simultaneously in Paperback by
Tower Publications, Inc., New York City
under title of *Concentration Camp, U.S.A.*

Sixth Printing — June 1978

Library of Congress Catalog No. 72-163851
ISBN No. 0-87026-026-X

PRINTED IN THE UNITED STATES OF AMERICA BY WESTERNLORE PRESS

ACKNOWLEDGMENT

The author is deeply indebted to the Library of the University of Arizona for allowing him free and unconditional access to the twenty boxes of archival material pertaining to the Japanese Relocation Camp at Poston, meticulously assembled by Dr. Edward Spicer, of the University's Anthropology Department, who served the camp as head of the Community Analysis Section, War Relocation Authority. In this priceless collection, pertaining to every phase of the colony, is the heartbeat of a brave and dignified people as they were put to the test. Especially is the author indebted to Dr. Robert K. Johnson, University Librarian; the late Dr. Rudolph Gjelsness, who so ably managed the Library's Special Collections Department; to Dr. Joseph Parks, the Library's Curator of Western Americana; and particularly to John Gilchriese, University of Arizona Field Historian.

To Everett G. Hager, historian of the Los Angeles Harbor area, goes special thanks for assistance in tracing the background drama of the Terminal Island and Fish Harbor expulsion. Without his timely aid it would have been difficult indeed to have reconstructed this unique moment of wartime history. And for an abiding interest in the evacuation tragedy, and for steering him into odd and little known facets of it, the author is especially indebted to his son, historian L. R. Bailey.

To such sympathetic and understanding Japanese Americans as Joe Nagano, George Tsuruda, who witnessed much of the evacuation firsthand; to Henry Mori, English language editor of the *Rafu Shimpo*, Nobu Shimahara, and those others who insist on remaining anonymous, but who lived out the life of Poston; the author acknowledges a very special debt. In opening their minds and hearts, they made this book possible.

CONTENTS

ILLUSTRATIONS

(Continued on Next Page)

ix]

ILLUSTRATIONS
(Continued)

INTRODUCTION

"REMEMBER PEARL HARBOR!" was the verbal thrust which tumbled the United States into a war for its survival, and remained the rally cry for as long as that vicious struggle persisted. To 127,000 Americans of Japanese descent, caught suddenly like ants in a vise, the slogan was just as shockingly persistent and compelling, but in a peculiar and different way.

"A day of infamy," President Franklin D. Roosevelt dramatically reminded the nation. But to Japanese Americans, who neither asked for nor wanted this sudden war, no more than did any other average American, the "day of infamy" had an ironic and tragic consequence almost unbelievable in retrospect. The roust of 112,000 Japanese people from the Pacific Coast during World War II, their detention in fifteen "assembly centers," their transfer and incarceration in ten immense concentration camps, represents an unsavory page of American history. It is not an affair often mentioned, and this nation, since it cannot point to the record with pride, would just as soon forget about it.

America is still hard put to justify or explain how a crime of such magnitude against a peaceful and law-abiding minority could have occurred in so democratic and easy-going a nation— a nation that claimed to be the melting pot of races and cultures— the hope of the world. Were its resident Japanese as vociferous and as hate-filled as other minority groups, a lot more would have been said and written about it; a few "Little Tokyos" might have been burned; and the average American would have been

11]

considerably less prone to consign this betrayal of a people into conscienceless oblivion. Quick to forgive, anxious and industrious about retrieving loss and honor, Japanese Americans have never given the nation the castigation it deserves. *"Shikata nai,"* they call it. Which is their way of saying: "What happened, happened. There was nothing we could do about it."

The only logical excuse so far advanced for this most illogical page of history is to blame it on wartime hysteria. Plenty of reasons were voiced at the time it occurred. Not one of these excuses—including sabotage, aid to the enemy, "fifth column," or lack of patriotism—has stood up under the caustic scrutiny of time and justice.

The "big roust" has no parallel in American history, unless one searches back to a little more than an hundred years before the "day of infamy." Then a likeness might be drawn—to America's expulsion of the Cherokees, the Chickasaws, the Creeks and the Choctaws. Once before, in America's earliest days, the nation moved another immense minority group. These Indians were forcibly expelled from homes, land, and the roots of family habitation. They were mature Indian nations that had been living in the east and south long before the white man set foot on this hemisphere. When America shoved these Indians far out to the western prairie, it was not wartime hysteria. White men simply needed and coveted the land. It was greed. A century later, Japanese Americans were to taste a little of this greed. It was mixed with the hysteria. In eviction and evacuation, there was historical precedence.

From the beginning the United States has taken immense pride in its role as a melting pot—the assimilating, catalyzing wonder machine of the world. Here peoples of different nationalities, religions and races are turned into citizens and patriots. America's door was always open; ever beckoning to the oppressed. But to say that those one hundred percent Americans who had already made the grade were not capable of hating, persecuting and discriminating against those only heading into the racial melt, would be to utter a palpable lie. Hate and discrimination, unfortunately, have been with the nation from its beginning. The black man knows this well; so does the ousted, defrauded, and slaughtered Indian. So does the Mexican national, who is noisily and violently reminding Americans of their racist attitudes in the Southwest. Mistreatment of Orientals, particularly the sad page of California history mentioned here, is something America is anxious to sweep under the rug. The record of discrimination against Orientals is long and painful.

Up to the year 1853, when Commodore Matthew Calbraith Perry sailed his American warships into Tokyo Bay, and at gunpoint forced Japan to open her harbors to trade and foreign intercourse, there was no such a thing, anywhere in the world, as a Japanese émigré. Japan's Shoguns had shut out the universe. The Japanese people, turned inward, were having nothing whatever to do with the greedy and turbulent outer world. This national isolation lasted for two hundred years. The America who forcibly opened Japan's doors, who shoved that nation into the strident Twentieth Century, would, less than a century later, be facing Japan's challenge in war.

Chinese were the first Orientals to come to America's shores. They were a part of the strange and swarthy peoples from many nations who swarmed into California with the discovery of gold at Sutter's Creek. White Americans, from 1849 onward, flooded California in even greater numbers. As usual, they considered everyone but themselves as foreigners. Even the Mexican-Californians, owners of the land being usurped, and natives of its culture, were termed "greasers," and viewed as interlopers. "Greasers" caught the same contempt handed out to Indians, Chinamen, Hindus, and Chileans. Plenty of racism came west with the Argonauts.

In California, the Indian fell first to the guns and greed of the Caucasian superpatriots who took over the province wrested from Mexico in 1848. The sordid tale of California's Indian extermination has had only fragmentary mention in America's history

13]

books. The running battle with the Mexicans took longer—but, in the end, was just as overwhelming and thorough.

What befell the Japanese Americans in 1941 had much of its roots in the anti-Chinese pogroms that began in the 1850s. Oriental immigrants who worked their gold claims in groups were slaughtered en masse by greedy miners who coveted or disputed their claims. When Chinamen began congregating in California's cities, many Americans vented their fury on these inscrutable heathens from another land. In Los Angeles a white man lost his life in dispute with a Chinaman. The pueblo's Chinese section was quickly overrun by alert citizens. Six Chinamen were killed in the first bursts of gunfire. Fifteen others—men, women and children—were summarily hanged from anything handy enough to support a rope.

In San Francisco, latent anti-Chinese sentiment broke out into violence in 1877; and fifteen California communities drove out their Chinese residents at gunpoint. The tumult swept up the Pacific Coast to Washington where, in the same year, Tacoma burned its Chinese quarter.

The racists were well organized. Politicians found the minorities, especially the Chinese, a handy whipping post for economic woes, and a never-failing vote-getter. California's Workingman's Party, dominated by the Irish, whose immigrant fathers had, a generation earlier, come under similar attack in the east, rose to dominant power on its cry of "The Chinese Must Go!" The Chinese, brought in by the thousands to build the railroads, stood as lethal threat to the Irish, who had considered railroad-building their own province.

From the beginning the workingmen and voters fought the Chinese. An incredible number of discriminatory laws against the "yellow peril" were passed, on city, county and state levels. In 1882, enlisting the help of southern states congressmen, California's representatives succeeded in pushing the Chinese Exclusion Act through the United States Congress. While this put immediate and effective stop to further Chinese immigration, the congressmen, in their eagerness to get the measure adopted, did make one real blunder. They failed to include the Japanese in their new law.

This was understandable because, at that time, the Japanese were scarcely thought to be a menace. Nipponese boys, from age fifteen to thirty, had only begun to arrive—mostly through the port of San Francisco. They brought with them no wives or children. English was a harsh and complex language, understood by few of them, and spoken by none. Hotel and inn keepers met the bewildered lads at dockside, used them as menials, or acted as employment agents—on commission—and hired them out for any kind of labor the bright and intuitive young men could do.

While the Exclusion Act failed to prevent the immigration of Japanese to America's shores, dozens of other laws were directed against these pollutants to the Anglo-white concept of national purity. Naturalization and citizenship privileges were withheld from the new arrivals. These first Japanese emigrants were the Issei generation.[1] In spite of economic obstacles, language difficulties, exploitation, and discrimination, they made homes for themselves along the Pacific Coast.

But the Japanese men desperately needed wives and homemakers. This want was uniquely filled by the "picture brides." Photos of eligible and willing girls were sent from Japan. For a fee, and after choice from a picture, a *nakadachi*, or go-between was appointed. The bridegroom picked up his picture bride at dockside in San Francisco or San Pedro. The marriage was quickly consummated. Rate of disappointment over this evanescent courtship could not have been too great, because, by 1910, the Japanese population in the United States, men, women and children, had risen to 72,157.

The Isseis, of course, were aliens, and became increasingly unwanted in the American body politic. But their children, by birth and Constitutional guarantee, were American citizens. Considering language, culture, and the many problems they were forced to overcome, the Japanese Isseis, up to the time of

[1]Those born in Japan were known as *Isseis*. The *Niseis* were second generation Japanese Americans, and are citizens.

Pearl Harbor, had made astonishing adaptation to the American way of life. They were most willing and anxious to integrate. Desperately they wanted to be a part of their newly adopted land.

The problem of Chinese incursion had been halted by the 1882 Exclusion Act, but now the Issei invasion was the new threat. Japanese, like the Chinese, were Orientals. Americans were never very adept at telling them apart. The mantle of hate, once so virulent against the Chinese, was quickly and securely fastened to the Japanese segment of the yellow peril. And, in California especially, it stuck.

Public outcry, and political oratory, never wavering through nearly a century, now at last caught up with the Japanese. In 1900 they were considered a threat. By 1930 they had become a sinister menace. Their numbers, according to the scaremongers, were increasing. Startling statements were made—the public was warned that their proliferation, in numbers, were as high as half a million. The danger they posed to labor, industry, and national security held continuous mention in the press—especially the California press. Long before Pearl Harbor, the newspapers—particularly the Hearst newspapers – were vitriolic in their attacks.

Organizations were formed to root out the problem. In 1906 Japanese children were excluded from San Francisco's public schools. Youngsters were forced to take classes in a claptrap schoolhouse bordering Chinatown. More national and state laws were passed. In the Ozawa Case, decided in 1923, the Supreme Court came up with the unique finding that since the Founding Fathers had never contemplated the presence of Japanese in this country, they were therefore ineligible for naturalization.

In 1913 California passed her Alien Land Law, which effectively prevented Isseis from acquiring or owning land. The politicians, however, were unable to plug all the loopholes. The American Constitution guaranteed the right of citizens to own property. Isseis simply purchased their land and fishing boats in the names of their Nisei children, who were citizens.

It was constantly prated that the Japanese, through their picture brides, were breeding like rabbits; that in a few decades they would outnumber the white population by sheer fecundity. The Japanese Exclusion League was formed. Patriotic societies, veterans' organizations, Native Sons and Native Daughters, took up the cudgel. V. S. McClatchey, wealthy owner of two influential California daily newspapers, retired from newspaper managing to head up the Joint Immigration Committee, to lecture, lobby, and campaign against California's Japanese. Like the Hearst press, his publications carried on a drumfire against the Japanese menace up to, and including, the war years.

It was inevitable that racial hysteria, so consistently pounded home by press and radio, would move public opinion to action. In 1924 Congress passed its Japanese Exclusion Act. Finally and effectively the doors were slammed shut to further Japanese entry into the United States—as had the Chinese Exclusion Act in 1882. Politicians, property owners, and propagandists could now breathe easier. Tide against the yellow peril was turning.

Of the ethnic groups coming to America's shores, only the Orientals were affected by these drastic measures. The Japanese naturally reacted with hurt and shock. The nation of Japan, beginning with Commodore Perry's brusque Naval incursion, had, by now, not only awakened to the Twentieth Century, but had blossomed with incredible swiftness into a world power. Already she was challenging America for control of the Pacific. Japan vociferously protested the Exclusion Act as an insult to her citizenry, and a national affront. Unquestionably the Act contributed to the development of strained relations between the two countries which, commencing with Japan's alliance with Germany and Italy, eventually ended in war itself.

By the time of the Exclusion Act the Issei males, and their imported brides, were middle-aged, and had only begun to rear their families. At the time of Pearl Harbor the Isseis were fifty to sixty years of age. Their children—the new generation, the Niseis —were mostly between the ages of seventeen and twenty-three. Here was a real generation gap. The youngsters, for the most part, were guiding the destinies of forty thousand older people, who had been born in Japan.

On the day the bombs fell on Hawaii, two-thirds of the nation's "yellow peril" were American citizens by right of birth.

A PORTION OF FISH HARBOR, TERMINAL ISLAND

This is an early view, about 1934. By 1941 the vacant area to the right had become the site of four additional fish canneries, and the Japanese community had grown into a city of three thousand population.

—From an old print.

CHAPTER ONE

On December 7, 1941, when Imperial Japan plunged America into World War II by its surprise attack on Pearl Harbor, Japanese Americans in the United States numbered 127,000—with 112,000 of them on America's west coast—most of them in California. By their unobtrusive industry, California's Japanese had by now established themselves as highly efficient and dependable farmers and horticulturists. Their vegetables and flowers, because of superlative quality, were in high demand. They carried their skills into California's market place, as merchants, hotel operators, and restaurateurs. In the seagoing fishing industry, their boats went out of Los Angeles Harbor to roam widely on the Pacific. They furnished the endless demands of the Terminal Island canneries. Their efforts brought fresh and refrigerated fish to America's tables.

Their children, American-born Nisei,[1] were a visible part of nearly every California grade school, high school and college—especially in the State's central and southern area. These Japanese Americans were good students. Their parents were good people—law-abiding, sober, and desperately anxious to shoulder their responsibilities as Americans. Their only fault—they wore the face of the enemy.

[1] To the *Nisei,* as American-born citizens, and *Issei,* their forced alien parents, was added a third group called the *Kibei. Kibeis* were American-born children who were sent to Japan for extended sojourn or schooling, and who had returned to the United States.

It took that suddenly erupted war to bring instant judgment on every human who looked like a "Jap." After that Sunday's tumble of bombs on Pearl Harbor, most Americans retched with hysteric hate and fury whenever they saw a "Jap." And little wonder. Japan's attack came with overwhelming suddenness. American defenses were completely unprepared. It commenced around 7:55 a.m., Honolulu time, with a thorough and furious air strafing of the Oahu military airfields—Hickham, Wheeler, Kaneohe, Ewa, and Bellows. The first thrust destroyed 188 American planes on the ground, about 159 more were so badly damaged that they could not be flown. Only 81 American planes were able to take to the air, and these were helpless against wave after wave of carrier-launched Japanese bombers and fighters who systematically demolished America's "bastion of the Pacific."

Ninety-six warships were tied up in Pearl Harbor that tragic Sunday morning. Eighteen of these were either sunk or rendered useless. Battleships *Arizona, Oklahoma* and *Utah,* and the destroyers *Cassin* and *Downes* were total losses. Battleships *California, Nevada,* and *West Virginia,* and the *Oglala,* a mine layer, were sunk, or beached—but later salvaged and repaired. Nine other Navy vessels took bombs with heartbreaking destruction, including the battleships *Maryland, Pennsylvania,* and *Tennessee;* the cruisers *Honolulu, Raleigh* and *Helena;* the destroyer *Shaw;* seaplane tender *Curtiss;* and the *Vestal,* a Navy repair ship.

The magnificent *Arizona,* pride of the fleet, blasted apart by a Japanese bomb in her forward magazine, carried her crew of 1,102 young Americans to a watery grave. The raid virtually wiped out America's Pacific air force and fleet. This wanton killing of 2,403 service men, and the wounding of 1,178 more, spun the American people into a state of shock. Their trauma swiftly catalyzed into frantic anger, then to hate, for the Japanese nation and its people. For the "Japs" had suddenly and overwhelmingly humiliated them in the eyes of the world.

The Hawaiian devastation was an instant reminder that Terminal Island, in California, and the Navy, Army and Marine bases at San Diego, San Francisco Bay, and Puget Sound, were equally vulnerable to sudden attack and invasion. Terminal Island, for instance, is very strategically located. It lies as the east wing of Los Angeles Harbor, and possesses a naval base equal in importance to that of Pearl Harbor. On that tragic morning, it also possessed a sizable population of "Japs."

Terminal Island's Japanese were mostly congregated in the quaint and picturesque community of Fish Harbor, fanning outward from the island terminus of the San Pedro ferry. The "bombing" which Fish Harbor was destined to receive may not have been so deadly as the one at Pearl Harbor, but to its townsfolk it was fully as soul-shaking and memorable.

From Wakayama Ken, in Japan, had come the original fisherfolk of Terminal Island. No one is sure about the exact date, other than that they were among the first American arrivals. And, almost up to the passage of America's and California's prohibitory alien laws, there had remained that familial trickle of immigration out of which grew the compact and isolated community.

Not all of Fish Harbor's three thousand inhabitants were from the old country, nor even a respectable fraction of them. The original settlers had sired many children through the years. Long before that evil hour in 1941, when Japan's sneak attack laid its black shadow upon the village, its Nisei count had far outstripped its Issei emigrants. It was the fishing fleet, and the canneries, which kept Fish Harbor alive and prosperous.

Fish Harbor had its restaurants, beauty shops, pool halls, and a hotel. It had its grocery stores and delicatessens. When its youngsters progressed from Terminal Island's own little elementary school into junior high school, high school, or college, they daily crossed the island ferry to San Pedro or the California communities beyond. To make a discernible step in anything, outside the world of fish and its processing, one always had to follow this same watery path.

Terminal Island poked like a finger up the Cerritos Basin into the ocean outfalls of Long Beach. On the northeast half of the island, where the narrower channel was bridged into Long Beach proper, stood the vast complex of Long Beach Naval Station, home port to many of those battleships and cruisers sunk and destroyed at Pearl Harbor. At the island's lower end was the Federal immigration and customs facility, and the low and fenced spread of Terminal Island Prison. The channel itself, between San Pedro, Fort MacArthur and the Lomita oil fields, bristled with the slips and quays of busy and vital Los Angeles Harbor. Here stood its shipyards, drydocks, and the oil storage tanks servicing the vast petroleum commerce out of one of the busiest and most vital harbors in the world.

Between the Naval Base and Terminal Island Prison sat Fish Harbor. Anachronistically adjacent to the Japanese community, its fishing fleet, and the fish canneries, was the plush and sedate Los Angeles Yacht Club. Here was mothered the sleek and shiny craft of Southern California's more opulent society.

On that Sunday morning of December 7, the Fish Harbor residents were busy with their usual chores. The women, many of them employed at the canneries weekdays, were making good use of their day off by washing clothes and cleaning their houses. The children, free of school duress, were happily at play on, Tuna Street, Cannery Street, the quays, and the boat yards. The menfolk had their motor craft far out beyond the breakwater. To these thrifty and ambitious *nihonjins*—when the fish were running—Sundays and holidays were like any other time.

Suddenly, out of an hundred Fish Harbor radios, came the stentorious announcement. Pearl Harbor was under attack. The nation was Japan. Ships were being sunk. The Hawaiian Naval Base, and Hickham Field were being destroyed. War, sudden and terrible, had come out of Asia.

President Franklin D. Roosevelt came on the air with his "day of infamy" pronouncement. Then followed the belated censorship—the fragmented bulletins leaking past only adding to the fright and speculation. For the remainder of that awful day the radio carried the commentary and postulation of analysts, congressmen, and suddenly resurrected Asian experts.

By afternoon the radio was reacting in violence against Japan and her treachery, and the Japanese as a race. To 127,000 Americanized Japanese, this Sunday was more than a day of infamy. Before it was finished, it had shaped up as a day of unmitigated tragedy. A time of frantic soul-searching. A black hour of worry and fear.

To Fish Harbor, and its citizens, this Sunday had started unusually tranquil and promising. It was one of those fair days, when the air was so clear that the breakwater seemed within swimming distance, and the blue-purple rise of Catalina Island loomed sharply visible out to westward. Before the day was over, the world was turned upside down. Fish Harbor was hourly gaining more reason to "remember Pearl Harbor."

For the remainder of that unholy Sunday, the people walked their little town with uneasiness and fear. The jovial, carefree, smiling faces were gone. Conversation was in whispers, furtive and frightened. And as the radios in the homes spewed America's indignation against Japan and its people, rumors, born in shame and uncertainty, began to convulsively seize the community. Over everything hung the pall of worry concerning Terminal Island's fishing fleet, out beyond the breakwater, in the Pacific, in the Catalina waters, with some of the larger units of the tuna fleet as far south as Panama.

As the afternoon progressed, things began to happen. Shore patrols from the Navy base—helmeted sailors with rifles—began herding the Fish Harbor residents off the streets, and into their homes. Jeeps, with armed Navy men, began patrolling the town.

Telephone communication in and out of Fish Harbor was suspended. The suddenly overloaded underwater cables from San Pedro had to be relieved to give full access to the Navy base and government customs offices. The residents, aware that they had become virtual prisoners, were uneasy and panicked.

Then the boats began arriving. "Fishing boats were coming home by hundreds! Eighteen years as an inhabitant here, but never have I seen such a sight! It was just like a flock of sheep being herded into their pens!"[2]

It would be days before the larger boats, far out to sea, would arrive at the slips and docks of Fish Harbor, but the smaller craft, apprized by radio of the fearful happenings, were coming into home port like a drove of locusts. With the Japanese residents already herded into their homes by the military, the landings were packed with Caucasians, anxious to unleash their fury aroused by the Pearl Harbor attack, and the anti-Japanese venom now spewing from every radio.

Decades ahead of this evil Sunday, the newspapers of California had hammered at the "yellow peril." For generations, books and writings had denigrated America's Oriental émigrés. Japanese acquisition of land, businesses, and fisheries, had seldom been viewed as the efforts of a hard-working, intelligent and thrifty minority attempting to build a decent American citizenry. Solid entrenchment of Japanese Americans into national commerce was a diabolical conspiracy. Japanese tuna boats out of Terminal Island, long-ranged, efficient, and modern, were, according to some of the more rabid columnists, manned by trained commanders from the Imperial Japanese Navy, with ranks as high as admiral.

Now, with Japan already drawing American blood, and the Terminal Island fishing fleet doubtless operated by Japanese fighting men disguised as fishermen, there was no holding back the hysterical mobs who met the first boats of the fleet as they pulled into the slips of Fish Harbor. Many a fisherman staggered home that tragic Sunday, bleeding and bruised from his beating by the superpatriots, his catch summarily confiscated, and himself bewildered and frightened by the strange reception he was receiving in his home town.

But this day was not over. "On the street, persons with whom we used to speak and joke, looked to me as strangers. It was very

2"The Evacuation of Terminal Island," by a Terminal Island Nisei. A written report in the Spicer collection of Poston papers, special collections department, University of Arizona Library. The interviewee in this document, probably for security reasons, was identified only by initial.

difficult to smile—nobody did! There were people talking in groups; there were people hurrying to and fro, all greatly disturbed. Soon the whole Island was filled with soldiers, machine guns, and jeeps. They started breaking up the chattering groups of people."[3]

The sailors from the Naval base were one thing, the Army's arrival from Fort MacArthur was another, but when agents of the Federal Bureau of Investigation arrived at Fish Harbor, things moved fast. Every house was ransacked for shortwave radios, cameras, signaling devices, and cryptic Japanese writings. *Kenjinkai* or Prefectural Association documents, and even proficiency certificates in Kendo, were confiscated. The ferry to San Pedro was closed to everyone with a Japanese face. Fish Harbor had become a prison.

Far into the night the agents hammered at the doors, and the Isseis were lined up and interrogated. Hundreds of the male population were hauled off to Terminal Island Prison. In their hunt for potential enemy agents, the FBI left nothing to chance.

Fish Harbor had the misfortune to be located center of the vital harbor, midway between an Army base and a Navy base, in clear view of the Navy's sudden mine-laying operations, and the greatest oil storage concentration in America. It lay much too close to shipyards and drydocks. Its people were operating a fleet of seagoing vessels. This town's bewildered residents were suddenly the most watched and feared group of human beings in the nation.

Until interrogations were completed, and the alien roundup finished, those who dared to come out of the house on Monday morning were hurried back in by the military guards. No one was allowed to board the *Ace* or the *Islander*—the ferries for San Pedro and the outer world of work and school—without clearance passes—and the passes were slow in coming. Stores were closed, by government fiat, as was every other business establishment in Fish Harbor. Boats were forbidden to leave the docks. Every man in town knew he was a prisoner.

[3]*Ibid.*, Poston Collection, University of Arizona Library.

Every male who had visited the homeland within recent years was permanently kept in custody. The stores remained closed day after day—officialdom apparently unaware that even a Japanese community required food and sustenance. Earning a livelihood was out of the question. There could be no more fishing. The canneries discharged everyone with an Oriental face, and hired Yugoslavs, Italians, and Filipinos in their stead. Before the week was out, principally through the efforts of the Japanese American Citizens League, clearance passes were finally issued to Niseis and others not under suspicion, so they could board the San Pedro ferry and go out into the world of school and labor.

The school children in attendance at San Pedro fared better than those attending colleges and universities in Los Angeles and beyond. Even worse discrimination was leveled at those who attempted to cling to their jobs in California's suddenly hostile world. Every employer with a grain of patriotism no longer allowed workers with Japanese faces in their sight—no matter how skilled or proficient they might be. Civil Service employees caught it along with the others.

No Japanese were safe on the streets of California's cities. Mob action and beatings were reported. Everyone with the wrong kind of face soon found it far more expedient to hide than to suffer the stares and snarls of people who once were unconcerned and friendly.

Pacific Coast Japanese-language newspapers and magazines ceased publication, either voluntarily because of fear, or by summary orders of the Office of Civil Defense. The Japanese language, written or spoken, was an inscrutable mystery to most Americans, and in the hysterical atmosphere of these first months of the war, the fact that it was incomprehensible, made it suspect.

The Japanese colonies and "Little Tokyos" of Los Angeles, San Francisco, Portland and Seattle, had overnight become repugnant and fearsome to the Caucasian citizenry. Their inhabitants hid indoors—furtive-eyed, bewildered, and frightened.

Wherever Japanese Americans were—on farms, in shops and stores, on jobs, and in school—they felt crushed by the sudden antipathy of their once reasonably friendly fellow citizens. But this hostility was nothing compared to what was occurring at Terminal Island.

The closed business establishments of Fish Harbor had become gamy with the stench of decaying food, and its people were desperate with want and hunger. In one instance, the wife of a delicatessen owner lived for days in the apartment above the store. Her husband had been hauled off by the FBI, and she was not permitted to step foot into her place of business. What food she had during her incarceration came from sympathetic neighbors willing to share. It had to be passed to her by string hoist through her upstairs window. All this occurred while downstairs stocks of perishable merchandise grew rotten and fetid.[4] When some bureaucrat in a panicked Federal department finally managed to press a button or utter a command, Fish Harbor's stores were once more opened for their essential purpose in the community. But the initial blunder was further compounded by the fact that the people's livelihood had been completely cut off. Fishing boats were not allowed to put to sea. All Issei Japanese bank accounts had been frozen and impounded. The Yokohama Specie Bank, the major depository of Terminal Island's fishing interests, had been closed and seized by Federal authorities because its home office was in the nation of the enemy. Most Japanese American wage earners had been fired from their jobs.

It proved a bleak and fearful December for Fish Harbor. On January 29 of an equally fearful new year, Francis Biddle, United States Attorney General, defined the strategic areas along the Pacific Coast, and followed it with an order for removal of all enemy aliens from these areas. Terminal Island was bound to be involved.

By that time six hundred male Isseis from Fish Harbor already were in prison,[5] and the Japan-born females were under constant surveillance. In Fish Harbor's population this averaged out to

[4]*Ibid.*, Poston Collection, University of Arizona Library.

[5]"West Coast Locality Groups," p. 6. Poston Collection, University of Arizona Library.

about one male prisoner for each family on the island. Fish Harbor had by now become a community of women and children.

The Nisei population—American born and American citizens —felt as imprisoned as if they had also been placed behind bars. In some cases they were worse off. No provision had been made for feeding a community cut off from jobs and livelihood, and under constant threat of rifle and bayonet. For the American educated Niseis, it was an imponderable action, and a bitter time.

"Several house-to-house searches were made by the FBI and unauthorized individuals. . . . Some of the FBI agents, the people report, were not courteous. The former customers and co-workers showed a great deal of hostility toward the Japanese. Japanese men were beaten by Filipinos and Filipinos beat other Filipinos who dared enter a Japanese store. The Slav workers at the canneries were belligerent and insulting to their former colleagues. Children were detained from attending school in San Pedro if they did not carry their birth certificates with them."[6] Fish Harbor could only groan and bleed, while it waited, tense and frightened, for the next blow.

It was not long in coming.

On February 13, a delegation of congressmen from the Pacific States urged upon President Franklin D. Roosevelt, as a necessity, the immediate evacuation of "all persons of Japanese lineage . . . aliens and citizens alike" from their Pacific-bordered States. Next day General John L. DeWitt, head of the Western Defense Command, alerted Henry L. Stimson, Secretary of War, to the necessity of this evacuation.

Five days later, President Roosevelt signed Executive Order No. 9066 into law,[7] authorizing the Secretary of War, or any command designated by the Secretary, to set up the necessary machinery and "military areas" for the summary removal of an entire segment of population deemed detrimental to the conduct of the war. On February 20, Secretary Stimson named General

[6]*Ibid.*, p. 7. Poston Collection, University of Arizona Library.
[7]Feb. 19, 1942.

DeWitt as the military commander responsible for carrying out the immense and far-reaching Order. Fish Harbor writhed in expectancy. Rumors of evacuation were constant and varied. The newspapers were bitter, denunciatory, and tireless in their demand for Japanese removal. The only friend and help through this mad and worrisome crisis was the people's own Japanese American Citizens League, who had set up a central organization in Fisherman's Hall, and were doing everything in their power to articulate and protect the people's rights during this time of hysteria. But other powers, far greater than theirs, were moving relentlessly upon the community.

From the beginning of the year rumors—to the effect that something drastic was to be done about Fish Harbor—had been afloat. Newspapers were screaming about the peril of a Japanese community sitting in plain sight of the anti-submarine nets and the Navy's mining operations at the Harbor entrance. It would be simple and easy, it was alleged, for these Japanese to signal and guide enemy craft through the unmined narrow channel, through the net opening, and on into the channel edging Terminal Island, to vital and vulnerable San Pedro, and to all the slips and basins of the great inner-harbor complex.

On February 14 the Harbor Commissioner announced that all fishing contracts, and all Fish Harbor rentals had been taken over by his department, and subject to cancellation at the end of thirty days. Reason given was that the United States Army was being put in charge of all areas of Terminal Island not held by the Naval base. Fish Harbor residents began talking seriously of the necessity of liquidating their holdings, and the eventuality of their having to seek residence elsewhere. The problem was that Fish Harbor now had become a community of women and children, the town's assets were frozen, all jobs were gone, and the boats impounded. There was no means at hand for such removal if and when it did come.

Ten days later American fears were crystallized. A Japanese submarine surfaced, just south of Santa Barbara, and brazenly shelled shoreline oil fields and storage tanks. "IMMEDIATE

EVACUATION OF JAPANESE DEMANDED," headlined the Los Angeles *Times* next morning. "Shocked by news of submarine gunfire on oil wells near Santa Barbara, Southern Californians yesterday demanded summary evacuation of all enemy aliens to inland points."

" 'We must move the Japanese in this country into a concentration camp . . . and do it damn quickly,' says Representative A. J. Elliott to the House. 'Don't let someone tell you there are good Japs. . . .' "[8]

As if that were not enough to shock Fish Harbor into paralysis, on Wednesday night, February 25, all hell broke loose. While residents of Fish Harbor cowered in the darkness of their homes, the night outside went wild with the howling wail of the air raid sirens, and was pierced and fingered by beams of searchlights nervously probing the sky.

Every antiaircraft battery from Fort MacArthur, and the Naval base, clear across fifty square miles to the mountains north of Los Angeles, suddenly commenced firing. The rattle and din, the shuddering windows, the crunch of shrapnel, brought sweating terror not only to the frightened citizens of Terminal Island, but to everyone in Southern California.

It was a profound relief to face a new day knowing that there had been no invasion. The morning newspapers and radio commentators were not at all certain there actually had been enemy planes overhead. Enough ammunition had been blasted skyward by the nervous gunners to have successfully stood off an attack.

Nevertheless, the possibility of seaward approach by enemy aircraft spelled disaster for the Japanese of Terminal Island. Late in the afternoon, on the same day, February 26, came the tremulous young Marines, knocking at every door. They were helmeted; rifles swung from their shoulders; they carried sheaves of mimeographed flimsies in their hands. The statement they handed each family, while fragilely concocted, swung the hard fist of authority. General DeWitt, under Order 9066, had delivered the ultimatum. All people of Japanese descent must be

[8]Los Angeles *Times*, Feb. 25, 1942.

off Terminal Island by February 28. That gave them only forty-eight hours to complete the removal.

The two days that followed were days of complete madness. Most of the Issei men, so essential in this grave crisis, were in jail, along with the more argumentative of the Nisei men. The entire burden of evacuation was thrown upon the shoulders of women, children, and those of the Nisei generation who had escaped the governmental dragnet. They had forty-eight hours to settle all their affairs, pack their belongings, sell businesses, boats and furniture, and leave the Island, their homes, and their town.

Harshly, and without mercy, the government had ordered them to move. Where they were to go, no one knew. No means of transportation had been provided by those who hurled the ban. No housing had been promised. Californians were in no mood to receive three thousand indigent and homeless Terminal Island Japanese—individually, or collectively.

"People were in panic. Businesses were sold at great sacrifice. In some cases, expensive equipment was destroyed by the owners who could not bear to part with them at the ridiculously low prices that were being offered. Junk men and non-Japanese neighbors swarmed to the Island, purchasing their furniture for practically nothing. Stealing was a frequent occurrence during these two days. The government did not provide trucks to move furniture, and many of the people did not have enough money to pay to have them moved, so they left them behind. The JACL was successful in obtaining fifteen trucks for the people's use, but this number was hardly adequate."[9]

The problem was exacerbated when California's press and radio announced that the "Japs" were being kicked off Terminal Island. The town soon became alive with bargain hunters and thieves. These buyers brought no hope or salvation. They had no interest in acquiring houses that were already marked for demolition. They were not going to buy expensive trawlers that

[9]"West Coast Locality Groups," p. 7. Poston Collection, University of Arizona Library.

31]

had to be left anyway, or purchase stores or businesses that once had prospered, but would prosper no more.

"We could not afford to lose a minute, and the hours passed away as if they were but minutes. For two days straight we worked without stopping. Was it two hours that we slept in all this time, or was it three? Too tired to think, we just dragged our tired bodies to bed around 3 a.m. without even changing our clothes, just to relax muscles and nerves, only to find that we had to drag our bodies up again as the alarm clock rang soon after . . .

"What really got me was the government [state] sales tax man who came around during the 48-hour rush, and who, with an expression of ease, sat down on the stool and started checking up our sales. Here we were working as if it was a matter of life and death, and he, without any respect for our precious minutes, came over and collected to the last penny. True, it was his duty to collect, but why couldnt he have done it later? . . .

"It was difficult to keep our tempers, although we tried hard. . . . For seventeen years, Dad and Mother had struggled mighty, mighty hard to build up their business. Every profit they made was put into the store for remodeling and improving it little by little. At the same time they were raising four tiny kids. . . . When they finally reached the peak of their business success and had nothing to worry about, when they finally succeeded in raising four children and sending them through high school and even one attending college—BOOM! came evacuation, and our prosperity crumbled to pieces.

"The precious 48-hours passed like a nightmare. The last night I took a final glance through the rooms in which we had slept and eaten ever since I could remember. With this unhappy emotion, I had to leave a once pleasant, cozy home. I wanted to cry, but my eyes were dry. Even now, my memories go back to my dear home, but never again will we be able to go back to it. . . .

"This was our last ride on the beloved soil of Terminal Island, once a hustling, bustling harbor; now, a ghost town. The only

[32

souls around were the soldiers and the prowlers who were going through the empty homes. . . .[10]

Typical of so many, this family lost home and livelihood overnight. Out of six thousand dollars in store-stock and furnishings, the family went off Terminal Island with five hundred dollars. What they could not liquidate at ruinous figures, was stolen, or distributed to other evacuees even less fortunate. To them it was one of the most merciless exoduses in history.

No government trucks ever showed up to haul the frightened and unhappy people they were expelling. But finally, from the ferry, and down Seaside Avenue, came a stream of vehicles belonging to Japanese farmers who were hurrying to the aid of their kinsmen from Terminal Island—trucks, family cars, every type of automobile, ancient and modern. Mingled with the cars piloted by men of Oriental countenance, were the fifteen trucks the Japanese American Citizens League had been able to procure, and a few vehicles and busses provided by the Baptists and Society of Friends. They were woefully inadequate to supply the demands.

Fish Harbor had closed itself out in a bedlam of confusion, with the military police looking on in stolid indifference. Children wailed as they hunted mothers. Women, fat with pregnancy, climbed into busses provided by the Quakers, for their transportation to Whittier, a town destined later to furnish an American president of Quaker lineage. The only males in evidence, to help load the trucks and cars, had been boys too young to be considered as threat to America's harbor defenses. These lads had worked willingly.

There was heroism everywhere—women and boys doing men's heavy work. There was a forced cheerfulness about it—the *nihonjin* way of hiding heartbreak. The *nihonjin* smile that masked the contemplation of suicide.

The wife of an incarcerated proprietor of one of Fish Harbor's billiard parlors was frantically drawing on the help of all

[10]See "The Evacuation of Terminal Island," pp. 8-9. Poston Collection, University of Arizona Library.

33]

women and boys on Tuna Street to aid her in lifting one of the heavy pool tables to the back end of a tiny Ford pickup truck. The only way the ponderous object would fit was to stand it up on' end. How the woman would manage the Ford aboard the ferry boat, with its low headroom—and what she ever would do with her pool table in California's no-man's land beyond the harbor channel—were riddles yet to be solved.

On the sidewalks were crates of rabbits, chickens, and cages of canaries and parakeets. The rabbits and chickens were already being covetously eyed by the half-starved evacuees. With a complete dearth of boxes and cartons, the women had desperately bundled their possessions in table cloths and bed sheets. One family had managed to drag their piano out to the sidewalk, only to abandon it—and those children adept enough to play *Chopsticks* or better were adding their tinkle of music to the confusion.

Many of the mothers had reverted to the old country way of carrying babies and small children on their backs. And wide-eyed little youngsters looked soberly and studiously at the strange world around them as their mamma-sans, either through denial or ignorance, joined the walking procession headed north to Cannery Street and Terminal Way, and the ferry that would dump them helpless and frightened into the hostile world of San Pedro.

That was the way, on this day, that the "Jap" menace on Terminal Island was abated. That was the end of Fish Harbor as a community. Their fishing fleet would never again put to sea under the expertese 'and captainship of the men who had brought their generations-old skills from the fishing provinces of Japan. Perhaps it didn't matter so much for the old people who were still alive. But it did matter to their sons, and their sons' sons, who were American born and citizens.

Americans in general, worried and preoccupied by a war the nation already seemed to be losing, sighed with genuine relief. The "Japs" had been kicked off Terminal Island. The submarines that had been sighted, and that had actually shelled the coastline, could not now be guided through Los Angeles Harbor defenses by enemy agents and aliens. If there was an invasion of this strategic area, there no longer would be three thousand "yellow-bellies" to welcome the enemy ashore.

But as to anyone giving heed to the plight of these evacuees, Fish Harbor women could only laugh bitterly, and cry out their frights. As they headed their loaded cars toward the ferry, they, like hundreds and hundreds of others, had not the slightest idea where they would lay their heads that night.

Someone in Washington had pressed a button, said a word, and their homes and community were no more. The government these people were pledged to—like Jupiter or Jehovah—could hurl down the decree, but cared not enough to provide a truck or a dormitory. A handful of loathed and hated "Jap" farmers, and a few feckless Christians, were the only ones who had responded to a little world in distress.

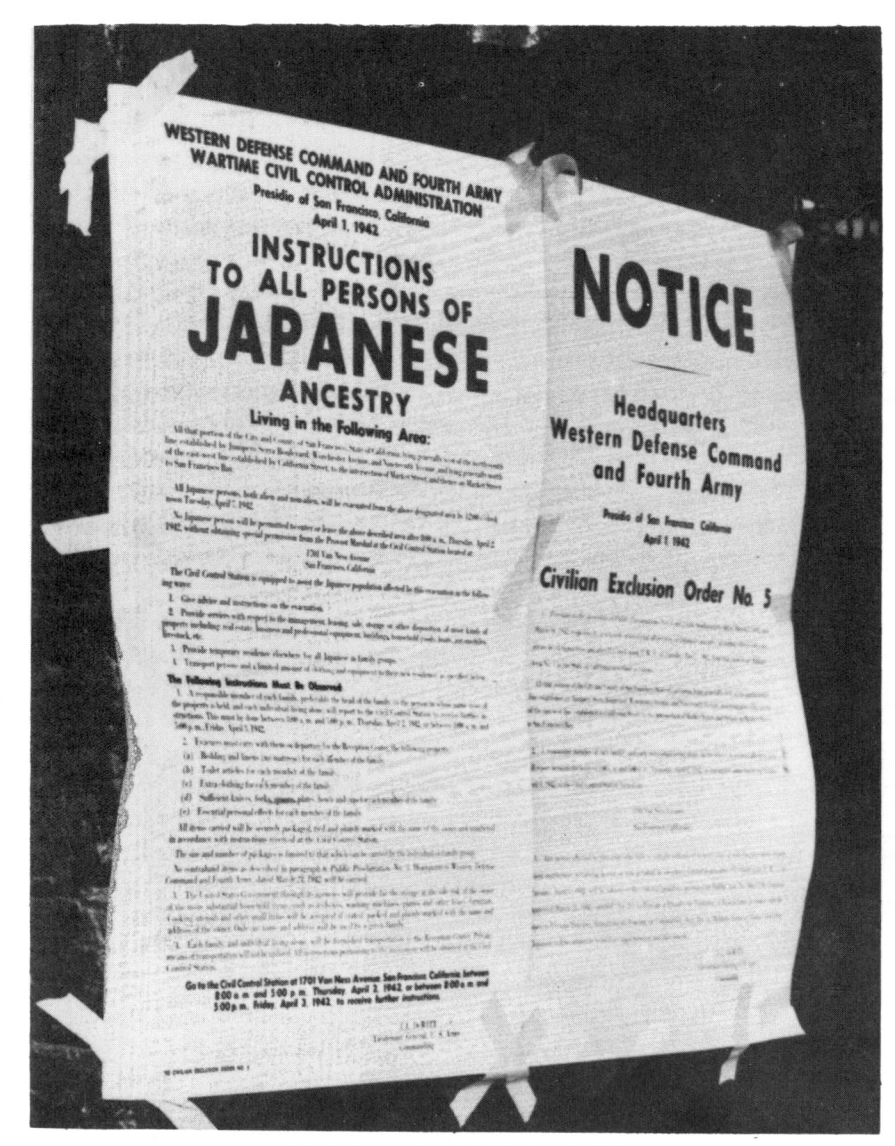

JAPANESE EXCLUSION ORDER

This order, posted in San Francisco, is typical of those prominently displayed in all other areas of the Pacific Coast. As noted, all Japanese people must be evacuated in less than a week's time.

CHAPTER TWO

WHILE the three thousand ex-residents of Terminal Island wandered as homeless mendicants through hostile Southern California, were interned in jail, or housed in whatever living facilities religious and welfare organizations could provide, things were moving relentlessly and fast against the entire populace of Japanese Americans on the Pacific Coast.

When Secretary of War Henry L. Stimson chose General John L. DeWitt to head up the Western Defense Command, he chose a man of vast energy and a penchant for getting things done. President Roosevelt's Executive Order No. 9066 gave DeWitt the sweeping authority he needed. On February 20 Stimson had not only named DeWitt as the military commander with full authority to carry out the evacuation program under Order No. 9066, but had declared the entire Pacific Coast as a strategic defense area.

DeWitt's Proclamation No. 1, on March 2, set up the western half of Washington, Oregon, California, and the southern portion of Arizona as military operations zones, from which all residents of Japanese descent must be removed. Japanese Americans in the more eastern states were not to be molested, since they resided in zones not militarily critical. Because the bulk of the Japanese American population lived in the Pacific states, the safety and security of their eastern brothers were strategically unimportant. But to handle the immense task of expunging the West's 120,000 occupants of Japanese ancestry, DeWitt, on

March 11, named Colonel Carl R. Bendetsen as Director of his Wartime Civil Control Administration. A week later Roosevelt's Order No. 9102 confirmed evacuation as national policy, by establishment of the War Relocation Authority.

Realizing at last how crassly they had botched the Terminal Island roust ("by February 28, 1942, all of the Japanese and Japanese Americans were evacuated from Terminal Island, but no shelter was planned or provided by the government"[1]) and how thoughtless and cruel had been the treatment of its victims, the new Authority named Milton S. Eisenhower as its Director. Mr. Eisenhower's first move was to aid the people who were forcibly removed from their homes by Executive Order.

By now the newspapers, especially in California, had shifted from pre-war criticism and hatred of its Asiatic populace, to shrill hysteria. They demanded immediate and complete removal. Navy and Army wives, returning mostly from the holocaust at Pearl Harbor, brought back to the States their tales of sabotage and "fifth column" activity. These rumors were later proved to be entirely false. But in these critical weeks, it took only these stories to intensify the fear that similar activities might take place along the vast shoreline of the West Coast. The shelling of a coastline oil field and the inexplicable "air raid" over Los Angeles were the final goads to action.

Even before Pearl Harbor there had been concern, openly expressed, regarding the immense farm acreage controlled by Japanese, and the wealth these thrifty people were accumulating in agriculture, commerce, and fisheries. Their California land holdings were estimated at $72,000,000. They included 5,135 farms, covering 226,094 acres—mostly in the San Joaquin Valley and along the coastal plain. Their other commercial interests were valued at anywhere between $55,000,000 and $75,000,000. For years covetous eyes had been turned on this growing affluence, and non-Japanese worries had been the concern of many an editorial column. But now, in the venom-charged air, abetted

[1]"West Coast Locality Groups," p. 8, Poston Collection, University of Arizona Library.

by historic prejudice against Orientals in general, there surfaced an ugly and brazen movement to forcibly appropriate this immense economic prize.

Even though the Japanese, both citizens and aliens, were circumspect in action, and kept themselves hidden as much as possible, there were cases of violence, intimidation, and attempted seizure of properties by overly patriotic and sometimes overly avaricious Americans in California and elsewhere along the Pacific Coast.

Paradoxically, some Americans also genuinely desired to protect the legal and social rights of this racial minority. Cautionary pieces in the press occasionally expressed concern over the imminent danger of a repetition of the hysterical outrages that had been directed against citizens of German descent in World War I.[2] Milton Eisenhower, with the newly established War Relocation Authority, hoped to minimize the danger of public violence against the Japanese. His job was to protect their rights as much as humanly possible, and at the same time eliminate the possibility of sabotage and enemy aid among a people who looked identically like the enemy. He quickly discovered that he was facing a formidable task.

The great Japanese roundup of 1942 was kicked off by "The Conference on Evacuation of Enemy Aliens," held at the Newhouse Hotel in Salt Lake City, on April 7. Present on this historic occasion were Colonel Carl R. Bendetsen, assistant chief of staff, Western Defense Command; Milton S. Eisenhower, director of the War Relocation Authority; Tom C. Clark, special assistant to the United States Attorney General; and Governors and Congressional Representatives from the various western states.

". . . I think, therefore, that these [Japanese] on the Pacific Coast, in the military zones, are potentially an enemy group," concluded Colonel Bendetsen at this conference. "They are law-abiding; they have not been guilty of overt acts. If they were

[2]See Carey McWilliams, *What About Our Japanese-Americans?* New York: Public Affairs Committee, 1944, p. 8.

aliens, they would be interned forthwith, or if they were American-born citizens they would be imprisoned. It is because of that potentiality that we have had to act to exclude them from that strip of Pacific Coast frontier where, in the event of attack, if our enemy were coming up the beaches, they would not be able to join hands with them. Therefore, as a matter of necessity to overcome that potentiality, it was necessary to provide that they be removed from that strip."[3]

Terminal Island had been purged of its "Japs." For a month, evacuation to other states, on a voluntary basis, was tried on California's unwanted population. Only a fraction of the people had responded. At the very time the Salt Lake conference was explaining and justifying the act, the vast removal was already on its way. It mattered not that the raging war had created an acute manpower shortage—it mattered not that Japanese Americans possessed skills and services essential to the war effort—no one was thinking how desperately workers and farmers and fishermen were needed. No one wanted to hire a "Jap."

So, the Army Corps of Engineers, in the amazingly short span of twenty-eight days, constructed shelters sufficient for one-hundred-thousand people in various assembly centers in California. There the "Japs" were to be interned until the greater camps, east of the mountains, or out of the Pacific area entirely, could be built to more permanently house them.

Most of the assembly centers blossomed-out on the handy acreage of race tracks, such as Tanforan and Santa Anita, and state and county fair grounds, such as the great one at Pomona. Manzanar Center had the unique distinction of being situated in an undeveloped area, far up the Owens Valley, with the mighty Sierra Nevadas between it and the populated and critical areas of Southern California. Started as an assembly center, it grew and matured to become a full-fledged and permanent concentration camp of long and lively history. But now, into these cities of rough pine and tarpaper were herded the bewildered

[3]"Conference on Evacuation of Enemy Aliens," Poston Collection, Box 2, University of Arizona Library.

"yellow bellies," torn from their farms, their jobs, their schools, and their homes. Many of the Terminal Island evacuees went to Manzanar. "They arrived when the center was being built, and suffered the privations of a pioneer newly constructed community. All of their experiences up to this time served to make them a bitter and discontented people."[4] Other ex-residents of Fish Harbor were herded into Santa Anita, along with the thousands of other Southern California citizens of Japanese heritage.

An attempt was made to soften the evacuation blow by calling Santa Anita a "reception center," but to the Harbor evacuees— even after their two months of furtive and impoverished existence in the hostile world of Southern California—the order was just as stark and brutal as the edict that had ripped them out of Fish Harbor.

Santa Anita, east of Pasadena, great and beautiful race track, playground of millionaires, was, like Manzanar, one of the earliest centers prepared for the preliminary processing and detention of California's Japanese. Orders for internment were brash, terse, authoritative. They were brayed over the radio, posted on brick walls, published in the newspapers. Santa Anita, to the homeless Islanders, was not chosen for its beauty. It was simply the closest and handiest place to turn one's self in.

Since many Terminal Island men had not yet been released from jail, the automobiles, following the long line through the sentry-guarded race track's outer gates, were mostly driven by women, and were heavily-burdened with the personal possessions they had been able to save. Speedily, efficiently, the cars were unloaded, and every bag and parcel tagged. Then the cars were surrendered, a receipt issued, and they were driven out to the vast parking area, to be impounded for the "duration." Most internees never saw their automobiles again.

Few Japanese Americans had any idea of what they would find at the "reception centers." All they were sure of was that

[4]"West Coast Locality Groups," pp. 8-9. Poston Collection, University of Arizona Library.

tersely worded order to report. Manzanar, located on the weather-swept west benchlands of the High Sierras, was hundreds of miles removed from the cities of the coast. So the Japanese Americans who were sent there had heard even less as to what it might be like. Those who moved into the Santa Anita Center were better informed. Santa Anita was located close to Pasadena and Los Angeles. The Los Angeles *Times* had already started telling of its glitter and reputation. Some of its articles were positively ecstatic in describing this wonder of the horse world:

"Multimillion-dollar Santa Anita race track—the world's most beautiful and luxurious racing plant—yesterday opened its gates as an assembly center for Japanese evacuees. Worried mothers with babies sighed with relief when they learned that farsighted Army authorities had provided them with facilities for warming milk for the feeding of infants. As nearly as possible, the evacuees will live lives as normal as can be arranged under the circumstances. They will have the freedom of the grounds. They can have the use of long-wave radios. They will have special recreational centers for both adults and youngsters. The kitchen will eventually be staffed with members of their own race, as will the hospital unit, with accommodations for more than 100 persons."[5]

What the internees actually found was an immense prison, complete with barbed wire fences, sentry towers with machine guns, searchlights, armed patrol cars, and helmeted soldiers packing rifles. They found long lines where they were vaccinated, interrogated, fingerprinted, and assigned badge numbers like prisoners of war. Those who had been born in Japan, and those still having difficulty with their English, faced cross-examination that was particularly long and painful.

What they found were endless rows of one-story tarpapered barracks, a veritable city of pine and paper erected on 420 acres of one of the race track's immense parking areas. But since the homeless Terminal Islanders were among the first to enter the center, they also found the barracks unfinished, windowless,

[5]Los Angeles *Times*, April 4, 1942.

doorless, and so far uninhabitable. When finally, after a day of "processing," and dog tired, the sad and disturbed evacuees were finally shown to their quarters, these, for many, turned out to be the stables, once home to the track's horses. The whitewashed cubicles were still redolent with the smell of creosote and horse manure. Seven humans had to share each stall unit of twelve by twenty-four feet. Their belongings, taken from the cars, and thoroughly ransacked for weapons, cameras, shortwave radios, and anything printed or written in the Japanese language, had been piled at the stall doorways.

Family beds were straw-stuffed mattresses in the whitewashed quarters, on an asphalt floor as hard as humanity's heart. Permeating everything was an aromatic effluvium that would have strangled anything but a horse. Those mattresses, provided for the occupants of the horse stalls, and to all other internees crowding into camp, must do until the "farsighted authorities" could scrounge from the War Department enough cots to give minimal sleeping facilities to the human masses they were herding into the race track.

Among the mutterings of the interness was the rumor of epidemics—that measles and influenza were already stalking the colony—and that the hospital building was as uncompleted as was the barrack city. But diarrhea—either from nervousness, eye-watering miasma, or the Army hash—was keeping the toilet facilities frantically busy—ten seats in a row—raw pine housing—automatic flushing every fifteen minutes. And the internees must wash in the common sinks and horse troughs, and eat at the field kitchen and outdoor tables until the six planned communal dining rooms could be set up.

There was no rest or relaxation in the congested little quarters; not even a lawn chair or bleacher seat had been made available. The internees walked aimlessly about the acres of their prison. Their feelings were the same as the other people they met—everyone looked frantically and unbelievingly at the high fences, the sentries, and the machine guns pointed inward to the compounds. Grandstand and infield area was off limits to

RECEPTION COMMITTEE, SANTA ANITA
A trainload of evacuees from Terminal Island, brought from San Pedro, via
Pacific Electric, to the assembly center at Santa Anita. The former race track
became a military prison to more than 18,000 Japanese Americans.

—Courtesy National Archives.

these first internees. Few things were ready. An overpowering fear was part of their first traumatic day. The months had been full of unbelievable frustration. Discovery and realization of this new betrayal was no easy thing to bear. It outraged their sense of justice—that American-born citizens could be treated as though they were the common enemy. It seemed incredible that the nation of one's birth could haul away a community's menfolk, summarily jail them, and then, on forty-eight-hour notice, drive their handicapped families from homes and livelihood. It was incomprehensible that American-born, American-educated Niseis could be herded like contaminated animals into this barbed wire concentration camp; to live like beasts in ill-provided and ill-conceived quarters that would have offended the most hardened criminal.

As the stream of evacuees funneled into Santa Anita internment center, its population swiftly mounted to a peak of 18,527 persons. In sixty days the race track became the thirty-second largest community in the State of California.[6] Its swift evolvement was matched by Manzanar, and the centers opened and operating at other race tracks and fairgrounds throughout the Pacific States.

Construction, at Santa Anita, somehow kept pace with the population increase. The stable area alone provided housing for 8,500 people. A barrack city was built across four hundred acres of Santa Anita's expanse; divided into seven districts. These districts were further subdivided into sections comprising the individually numbered buildings—all of pine and tarpaper—all monotonously alike. At first the streets were either numbered, or given a letter of the alphabet. But the internees swiftly and good-humoredly changed that. To them, the vast prison became "Japanita," a facetious contraction of "Japan" and "Santa Anita." Their incarceration was the "Nipponese Race Meet." Alphabetically streets were renamed Azucar, Bay View, Challedon, Discovery, Equipoise, etc.—after the race horses who had once

[6]*Pacemaker*, Santa Anita camp newspaper, issues of May 1, 1942 and June 2, 1942.

SANTA ANITA ASSEMBLY CENTER

A portion of the barrack city erected on the vast parking areas of the race track. The horse stables were also converted into housing for eight thousand additional evacuees.

immortalized the track.[7] The barracks themselves soon bore such signs as Burlap Row, Dusty Inn, The Jernt, etc.

Army field cookery vanished when the six separate mess halls were established in the various districts. They were marked and known to the internees as the Blue, Red, Green, White, Orange, and Yellow Messes. Each internee was issued, and must wear, the colored button that admitted him or her to the designated feeding station. As Japanese cooks took over the kitchens, the stale bread, potato hash, and coffee, dished up from Army mobile kitchens, were replaced by foods and dishes more in line with Japanese dietary tastes. Rice, vegetables, fish, meat and tea were served by dainty and gracious *nihonjin* young women, glad to earn the eight dollars a month the government paid to line-workers.

Diet stations were established for those internees who had medically restricted diets, and for babies and children requiring special formulas. At last the laundry buildings were operative—though the long lines of women waiting for their turn throughout the history of the camp indicated that the laundry facilities were never adequate. It took considerably longer for a library, hospital, visitation center, and social halls to be built. But even these eventually materialized.

Though anger and hurt smoldered deeply in their hearts, the people in every center accepted their lot with willingness and cooperation. The Army found no difficulty in recruiting workers to assist in the daily functioning of the vast enterprise. The monthly pay was $8.00 for unskilled and semi-skilled labor, $12.00 for skilled workers, and $16.00 for professional and supervisory performance. It was eagerly accepted—for many a once prosperous family had been reduced to poverty and helplessness by the sudden and drastic evacuation edict.

Competent Japanese physicians serving Southern California had been just as ruthlessly rounded up and interned as had the farmers and the fishermen. Their lucrative practices gone, they accepted without hesitation the responsibility of staffing and

[7]*Ibid.,* June 24, 1942.

manning Santa Anita's crude hospital, dental and out-patient facilities. Their task was enormous and all-consuming. Their pay, as working prisoners, was the top sum allowed—$16.00 a month. During the whole time that Santa Anita operated as an incarceration center, its medical facilities functioned without Caucasian supervision.

The *nihonjin* medical staff included trained and competent registered nurses—now lost to California's more fashionable hospitals. These dedicated souls labored for months, twelve hours a day, seven days a week, with twenty-four hour duty every fifth day. Besides coping with the recurrent diarrhea and influenza epidemics, and the ordinary accidents and illnesses of a fair-sized city, the nurses, doctors, and technicians cared for an average of seventy-five bed patients a day. With chronic shortage of equipment, instruments and supplies, they did surgery of every class and description, and delivered a crop of babies—nearly every girl child being given the name of "Anita." The first major operation was an appendectomy performed on a sixty-year-old woman from Terminal Island.

Bitterness or personal hurt did not thwart the internees in their united effort to turn their big prison into a smoothly functioning city. There was no civil disobedience, there were no pro-Japan rebellions, there was no sabotage. Everywhere was evidenced a universal willingness to cooperate, no matter how shattering their experiences of the recent past.

The Santa Anita internees were permitted to publish a small mimeographed newspaper—provided it was printed in English. Written communication in Japanese was not allowed. All of California's Japanese language newspapers had been closed down by military fiat, and the ban now just as rigorously enforced by the newly functioning War Relocation Authority. Out of Unit 5, Barrack 36, came the Santa Anita *Pacemaker*—bi-weekly, distributed free of charge.[8]

[8]See Anthony Lehman, *Birthright of Barbed Wire,* pp. 57-59 and *passim.* Los Angeles: Westernlore Press.

It was edited by Japanese American journalists, headed by Kaz Oshiki. On its staff was Chris Ishii, a former Disney artist—who lightened its pages with his "Li'l Neebo"—a cartoon caricature of a little Nisei boy, with buck teeth, shock of unruly hair, and a rakishly tilted Sant Anita jockey's cap.

Crude and inadequate though it was, the internees appreciated their camp newspaper because, insofar as rigid wartime censorship would allow, it expressed their own thoughts. It was staffed by *nihonjins*, and reflected the Japanese American point of view. It was no substitute, of course, for the vanished language newspapers. The Issei old people especially missed these Southern California publications, which, journalistically, had been of high quality and excellent and perceptive reportage.

California's Japanese had long ago come to view the state's big chain dailies, and the sycophant and gutless lesser sheets, with a jaundiced eye. For a decade preceding the war these newspapers had openly and blatantly conducted a vendetta against the "yellow peril." Not one newspaper had spoken out against the Terminal Island roust. Not one Los Angeles daily had concerned itself with the fact that the pogrom had been martialed against a racial minority, eighty percent of whom were American-born, American-educated, American citizens in every sense of the word.

With speed and efficiency these 120,000 Americans with the wrong kind of faces were herded into the fenced and guarded "reception centers." The necessity to provide work for this tremendous pool of idle people was quickly apparent. The vast majority had been harshly dumped from meaningful jobs. Positions for cooks, table waiters, janitors, and clerks were quickly filled—there were thousands of willing hands; an eager and frantic surplus. Santa Anita's work-project was camouflage nets, and it was given high priority. The Army Quartermaster Corps managed to get a modestly-sized factory installed under the race track grandstand. Carefully screened workers, of unquestioned loyalty and patriotism, were recruited for its work force. That, of course, meant employment only for American-born, English-speaking

GUARD TOWER, SANTA ANITA

Overlooking a portion of the stable area, converted to human habitation.

—*Courtesy National Archives.*

Nisei. The Issei old people, who conversed in native Japanese, or had difficulty in speaking or understanding English, were considered suspect. As aliens, they could not participate in the manufacture of so vital a wartime necessity as camouflage nets.

Internees who qualified for the camouflage net factory found their job strangely different from such previous occupations as farming, shop-keeping, and fishing. But it was "defense work," paid eight dollars a month, and saved one from clawing the walls in boredom and frustration. The task was to weave colored burlap strips into vast areas of chicken wire. Because the big room under the grandstand was so poorly ventilated, and so full of choking rag dust, employees were forced to wear surgical masks for every hour they worked. Also, the brightly dyed stripping the workers handled brought rashes and irritation to the skin. But, however distasteful and unpleasant the job, it was still meaningful work. To boost morale, "netters" were constantly reminded that they were aiding the war effort. As the patriotic elite of Santa Anita, they were issued cards granting them priority in the chow lines, and other special privileges.

When Santa Anita's grandstand and infield were at last opened to the internees, there was less aimless walking for the older folks. The grandstand could now be used for drama, recorded concerts, an occasional movie, and patriotic rallies. Since agriculturists made up the majority of the internees, the spacious infield was turned into an immense vegetable garden—a real boon to the constant demands of the six mess halls. Some of the internees who were not content with this larger communal effort, planted their own "victory gardens" alongside their barracks, the stables, and along the parkways and flower squares. Only the great racing oval, the immense grandstand and bleacher areas, and the pari-mutuel windows were reminders that this busy city had once been a playground of privilege.

Of all the "reception centers," Santa Anita was probably the most adaptable and workable. Its extensive acreage was flat and lent itself well to the housing demands for nearly twenty-thousand people. The railroad spur, built to service the horses

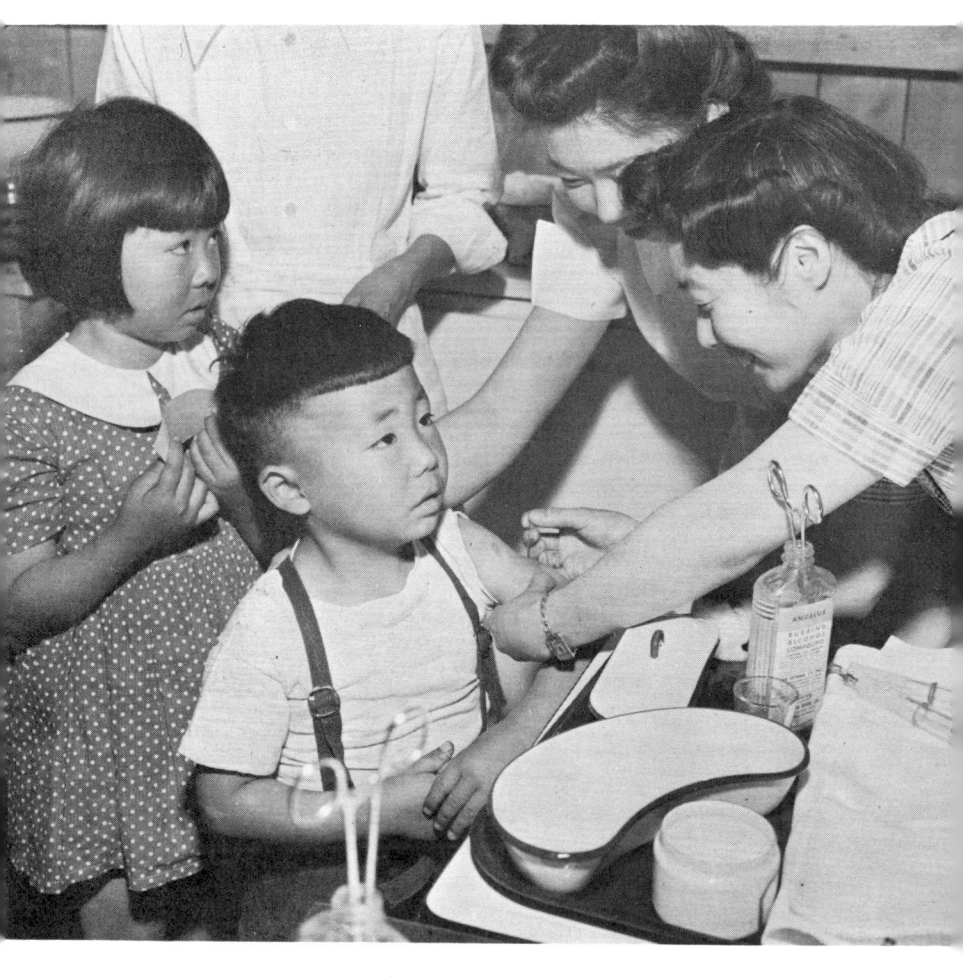

MEDICAL LINE, SANTA ANITA
A thing of fright, mystery and pain to the Japanese children.
                                        —*WRA Photo, National Archives.*

and public, now served the War Relocation Authority. It was used to bring in evacuees, a considerable amount of lumber, food and supplies. In all, sixteen assembly centers had sprung into active operation. They served as a gigantic holding operation until more permanent and secure disposal could be provided for every person of Japanese descent who were unfortunate enough to have lived within a strategic area of the Pacific Coast. Besides the racetracks and fairgrounds, a livestock exhibition area, a former mill site, and an abandoned Citizens' Conservation Corps camp had been utilized. But all had one thing in common—they were prisons. They had Army guards. They were circled with barbed wire.

California's centers were: Santa Anita, Tanforan, Pomona, Fresno, Manzanar, Marysville, Merced, Pinedale, Sacramento, Salinas, Stockton, Tulare, and Turlock. Oregon's center was at Portland. Washington's was at Puyallup. The center at Mayer served Arizona—and the Mayer center existed for the shortest amount of time—it lasted for only twenty-seven days. Santa Anita, with the largest population of any of the camps, was in operation longer than any of the other camps—seven and one-half months.

The roundup and detention of more than one hundred and twenty thousand people was a testament to Army coordination and engineering. The construction of vast tarpapered cities—already within sight of accomplishment by the War Relcation Authority—and into which the "reception centers" could dump their internees—was an even greater miracle.

Every internee in the sixteen camps awaited with worry and terror the next big removal. Attempts were being made to ease the burden and pressure. Frantic efforts were made to place Japanese students, especially at college level, in eastern schools. Willing and eager workers were offered to fill jobs far removed from the sensitive military area of the Pacific slope. The problem was, nobody in America wanted people with Japanese faces—as students, neighbors, or fellow workers.

53]

MEALTIME AT SANTA ANITA

It required six mess halls to feed 18,000 internees, on a per diem budget of less than fifty cents per person.

Some of the brightest young Niseis did find acceptance into eastern colleges; some of the former shop owners and agriculturists did find uncertain job positions far inland. But in point of numbers, this more humane plan fell far short of what was hoped. Farm laborers, those Japanese willing to toil in the sugar beet and potato fields of Idaho, Montana, Utah and Colorado—where farm labor was acute and desperate—had the most luck. Farmers, with unharvested crops, could stomach even a Japanese face, if a pair of skilled and willing hands went with it.

But the shock of the imminent new removal could only be an anticlimax to the diabolical horror of the first big roust. Nothing again could equal the unbelievable and unexpected suddenness of being uprooted from home and sustenance, to be herded like animals into military compounds, to queue in lines for food, interrogation, and every vital need, and to suffer all the hardships and humiliation that went with rejected and hated citizenry. The new camps could not be worse than these sixteen assembly centers. There was some possibility they might even be better.

Millions of feet of scarce and precious lumber were being diverted from civilian construction and military needs to build the ten huge camps now going up in various western states. Thousands of desperately needed workers were feverishly toiling to erect prison compounds to house thousands upon thousands of other skilled and desperately needed workers. The grim humor of this travesty seemed to be appreciated only by the internees themselves.

Manzanar, in California's Owen's Valley, safe and secluded behind the high barricade of the Sierra Nevada, was being expanded from holding center to a city of barracks and barbed wire. Tule Lake, inland, in the remote northeast corner of California, was under fast and heavy construction — to house the northern Japanese, and later, the incorrigibles, and those Isseis, Niseis and Kibeis who showed mental leanings toward Japan and the emperor.

At Heart Mountain, in Montana; Topaz, in Utah; Minidoka, in Idaho; in Colorado, Arizona, and as far east as Arkansas, the

MILITARY GUARD ALONG THE BARBED WIRE
As a "reception center," Santa Anita was under constant Army surveillance.

—*WRA Photo, National Archives.*

feverish building was going on. Ten city-size concentration camps were being readied as fast as the "reception centers" emptied, and sent the internees on their way. The miracle was how all this was accomplished in parallel with the acute necessity of simultaneously building barrack facilities for the greatest army of fighting men America had ever been called upon to field. The Fish Harbor families were not allowed full stay at Santa Anita. Many, before them, had been sent on to Manzanar. This camp, in Owen's Valley, had become favored by the internees—principally because, even though isolated, it was still in their beloved California. Tule Lake soon held attraction only to those whose sympathies were with the enemy, whose allegiance remained with Japan, and those who were so embittered by the evacuation that they no longer trusted the American government or its people. Interrogation was weeding out the unregenerates, but even so, it was evident that Tule Lake would not be one of the larger camps.

No one had any real choice as to where they would be sent. The WRA made full decision as to the future home of the population mass under their control. In July began the first human shipments to Arizona.

By that time those Terminal Island menfolk who had been "detained," had been released from jail or custody. Their hearings, after months of detention, had been quick and farcical. Now, at last, they were free to join their families in moving to whatever permanent camp the government was deciding they should go. Many of the male prisoners came out sullen and embittered by the experience of being jailed while businesses, jobs, and families were torn asunder. The more vociferous protestors quickly found themselves and kin shuttled on to the growing recalcitrant colony at Tule Lake.

At Santa Anita and the other Southern California centers there was much feverish talk about the Colorado River Relocation Center. Of all the camps, this was rumored and reported to be the biggest; the finest. It was being built in three immense units and, unlike the suffocating atmosphere of "Japanita," it was to be an honor city. Most internees pictured the Colorado River in the aura of Grand Canyon, white water boating thrills, and scenery and things that conjured up thoughts that were adventurous and romantic. Next to Manzanar, which was still in beloved California, most internees hoped and prayed for the Colorado River Center. It couldn't be worse than Santa Anita. One thing was certain, the internees were being siphoned out of Santa Anita as fast as bus and train could carry them. Those departing by rail moved out from the race track's private spur. The first ones shipped to the big Arizona camp were carried there by bus convoy. Later, when processing facilities became more efficient, the families were transported by rail to Parker, Arizona, and then shuttled by bus to the Colorado River camp.

It was a July morning when the first of the Arizona-bound internees filed out to the long line of busses that would take them to their new home. Who determined the mode of transportation, no one knew. The departure was a sad and silent one, because these pilgrims had no idea what to expect from Arizona. They knew now, for certain, they were not bound for the California camps of Manzanar and Tule Lake. The morning was one of mist and gloom, and the air so laden with its mixture of fog and industrial smoke that it pained the lungs, watered the eyes, and closed out even the near view of the towering Sierra Madres to the north. Santa Anita may have been the most beautiful race course in the world, but all of its green comeliness seemed lost in this morning's bitter and acrid haze.

All boxes and luggage, once more carefully repacked, had been tagged for "Poston"—to be sent on by special trucking or railway. Allowance for the journey was whatever bags or hand cases that could be conveniently lugged aboard the ancient vehicles commandeered by the Army. No one could ever have imagined there might be nostalgia in leaving "Japanita." But somehow, even on this gloomy morning there was, for many, a fleshly tug and a remembrance. Humans were like the chrysanthemums in California's thousands of little Japanese gardens—sink roots for half a year, and any spot on earth held affinity.

Fenced and guarded though it had been, with all the discomforts and stigma of prison, Santa Anita was still pleasing to the eye, and a definite part of their beloved state. There *had* been some good hours here—with family and friends sharing the stress. No one who had lived out their term at Santa Anita would ever forget it.

Military guards herded the last stragglers aboard the throbbing busses. One by one the big vehicles peeled out—through the circular drive, out through the sentried gates, heading east on Highway 66 toward the great new camp in Arizona.

AN AMERICAN CITIZEN OBJECTS TO IMPRISONMENT

This veteran of World War I vociferously objects to the reliquinshment of his automobile and possessions as he is herded like a common criminal through the sentried gates of Santa Anita.

—*WRA Photo, National Archives.*

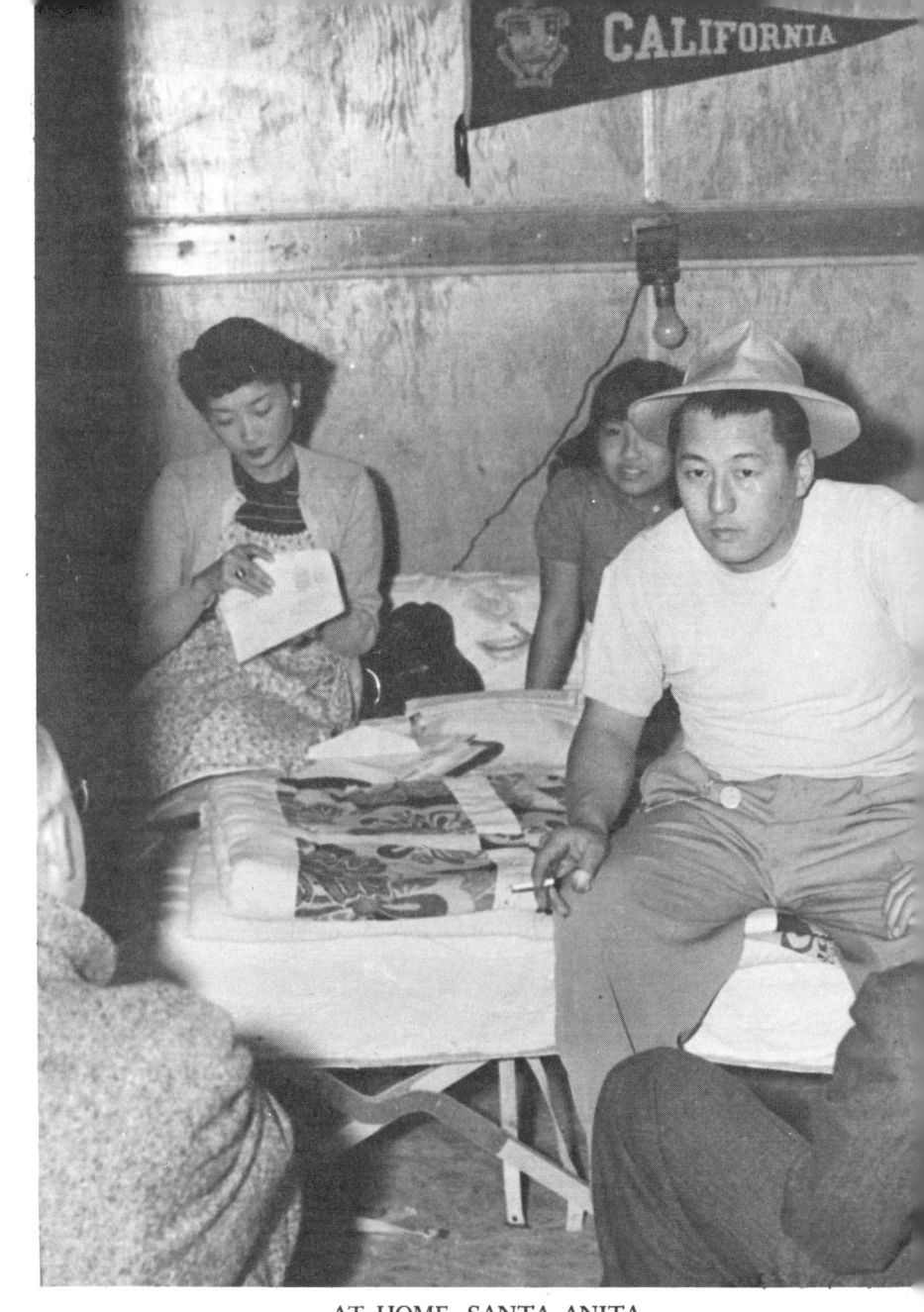

AT HOME, SANTA ANITA

A reconverted horse stable is the apartment of this cultured and educated family of Nisei American citizens.

—*WRA Photo, National Archives.*

CHAPTER THREE

To AMERICA as a whole, engrossed in bitter struggle for survival as a nation, the matter of Japanese relocation had become an item of minor concern. These people had been cleared out of the strategic and sensitive areas of the Pacific States. One could walk the streets of Los Angeles now without seeing a Nipponese face, and that was good. Out of sight—out of mind. There could be little empathy with anyone who wore the face of the enemy—American citizen *or* alien. The war was going badly. There had come ugly news—of Bataan's fall, and the retreat to Corregidor of the American forces in the Philippines. The Japanese Navy seemingly held clean sweep of the Pacific west of Hawaii. Other than the earlier naval victory at Midway, and the reckless token bombing of Tokyo, Kobe and Yokohama by Major Doolittle's carrier-launched bombers, there had been little good news out of the war to counter the series of stinging defeats since Pearl Harbor.

But to the remaining 110,000 Japanese Americans being hauled by bus and train out of the assembly centers to the relocation camps, the war had an eerie side to it, unknown and as yet incomprehensible to America at large. To them, evacuation had been a calamity. Most of them felt that the act, born of fear and hysteria, had been totally unnecessary.

The hardships they had suffered, involving property, kinship, health and future security, had been unwarranted. Friendships had been severed; homes torn up. They had been reduced to poverty—and to a proud and resolute people, the role of mendicant stood as a disgrace and a dishonor. Most of them were convinced that patriotic necessity for their removal had served as a convenient cloak to hide a long-standing hope of certain avaricious interests to rob them of their birthright. They were not blind to the fact that they had become objects of ridicule, public scorn, and exploitation. And they had no means whatever of fighting back.

They were saddened that the American government had failed to give them, as citizens, the protection which was their right. In the Terminal Island expulsion, officialdom had proven to be unreliable, inefficient, and with no shade of consistency. The FBI, by widespread and unwarranted arrests of the menfolk during the critical period of forced removal, had worked immeasurable hardship on families by robbing them of essential leadership, and leaving them prey to the patriotic predators who had descended upon their hapless dependents in a time of incalculable stress. Thievery and opportunism had been rampant and unchecked.

The assembly centers, widely touted by the press and radio as for their best interests and protection, had been prisons in every sense of the word. Throughout this temporary incarceration, the Nisei menfolk had continuously offered themselves as recruits to the Army and Navy—desperately hoping that by this gesture alone they might prove both citizenship and loyalty. Yet even in the frantic draft calls and recruitment for the armed forces, they had been repeatedly denied this final and fundamental right to serve the nation of their birth.

It was not always thus. Before Pearl Harbor, the draft calls and recruitment campaigns had caught up hundreds of Nisei boys. In Hawaii, long before bombs had ripped the Islands, the Army had its 298th and 299th Infantry—National Guard outfits, Nisei Japanese almost to a man. The Army now found itself stuck with a lot of "Jap" soldiers. It didn't quite know how to use them. And it wanted no more Nipponese regulars in its ranks.

Denied, defrauded, and disgraced—rejected by their fellow citizens—conveniently tucked away and forgotten—the assembly centers had become hell holes of despair and frustration. Now had come the relocation camps—prated to them as for their good, their duty, and their share of the war effort. In the case of many California Japanese, it was the Colorado River Relocation Center, near Parker, Arizona.

The great camp, being built in three community units, had been named Poston—in remembrance of Charles Poston, revered pioneer, and "father of Arizona." It was located on tribal lands of the Mojave and Chemehuevi Indians, and therefore geographically at least, under the thumb of the Indian Bureau. But while it was near the Colorado River, it was not directly on it. Of the ten great camps abuilding, the WRA had located Poston in a wilderness of desert, in the flat basin east of the river, geographically midway between Blythe and Needles, and in one of the hottest and most arid spots in America. Charles Poston, just and farseeing pioneer, were he alive, would have probably disowned the barrack city of tarpaper and pine, rising in the desert where he had once chased Indians, and now was named in his honor.

The long line of busses, after leaving Santa Anita, and loaded with this summer day's shipment of internees, ground its way toward the new home in Arizona. Once outside the cooling fog of the coastal basin, the journey, in the heat, became tedious and fretful. People groaned in their anguish, babies wailed in discomfort, and the children brawled as the miles of Route 66 thumped monotonously toward San Bernardino, and over the Redlands rim toward the desert in summer. As could have been expected, the busses were too ancient for air conditioning. All the travelers could do was shut eyes, listen to the whine and thump of the tires, and wonder about their new home to come.

Other than rest stops at San Bernardino and Banning, while the local townsfolk stared with wonder and hostility on the lines of Japanese people queued up patiently at the service station toilets and Coca Cola machines, the journey was pushed steadily until they reached Indio, in the insufferable heat of the Coachella Valley. At Indio's fairgrounds an Army kitchen had been set up for the Japanese caravan. There they dined on anemic corned beef hash, Mexican boiled beans, and washed it all down with sugarless tea and coffee. For children under ten, milk had been provided.

Then back to the bus, where the passengers worried, after taking on liquids at Indio, and as the oven-hot desert flung past, whether they could hold out to the next rest stop. It proved an immensely long and dry haul from Indio to Blythe; a time of testing across the arid earth.

At Blythe, after relieving themselves, and washing the sweat and grime from their flesh, they were allowed an hour's respite. Here they were issued sandwiches and coffee from another of those damnable Army mobile kitchens. With meat in wartime's short supply, the bread was held together with a slim shim of either cheese or peanut butter. In wearied silence they munched their sandwiches and drank their coffee, clinging to whatever shade they could find from the late afternoon sun.

Blythe was full of soldiers. One couldn't help but observe them, because they eyed the evacuees warily, as though they already were looking upon the enemy. It was explained to the nervous travelers that the soldiers of Blythe, who hovered in questioning wonder about the giant caravan of Japanese, were being trained, under command of General George Patton, for desert warfare, under desert conditions.

When the horns of the busses had again started yawking, the evacuees once more climbed wearily into their hot and humid vehicles. With the lowering sun, they were on the move again, and the hundreds of Japanese disappeared from the curious view of the soldiers and townsfolk of Blythe.

Not until they had crossed the Colorado, and had wheeled into Arizona, did they get their first stark reminder of the future home to be. Now they turned off the pavement to follow the river north, over a road that was little more than dust and ruts. The vociferous ones began grumping out the disgust they all were feeling.[1]

[1]Later, as facilities improved, and the WRA system better coordinated, more of the internees were moved to Poston by railway—from Los Angeles to Parker, Arizona, and thence by shorter bus haul south to Poston Units I, II, and III.

It was night before they got their first view of Poston Relocation Camp. What they could see was not too much. For those who had hoped for more, a single look was enough. First thing for certain, on entering Poston, was the gate. Here too were the sentries, the searchlights, and the guard towers. As they were beckoned through by the soldiers with rifles, cries and angry snarls filled the busses. Poston was no city of hope. Credence and assurance to the contrary, Poston was another concentration camp. To every weary person who entered, it was a prison formidable enough to frighten a leather-hided criminal.

In the hot night air, they stretched their cramped muscles, and tried, in the darkness, to gain better view of their new home. Every dream of creature comfort, held through the long journey, was quickly dispelled as the people were herded from the busses into the lines of waiting humanity—the damnable queues that had been their lot from the black days of Fish Harbor and on into Santa Anita.

But this time it seemed indescribably terrorizing. The feeling was one of crushing betrayal. What hadn't been told at Santa Anita was that the WRA had set this camp in one of the hottest deserts in America.

To weary evacuees the time seemed interminable before they had worked their way through the line to the wooden processing shed. There, under the lights—diffused by immense swarms of gnats and moths who left their glare and heat only long enough for target-drives to eyes and nostrils—it was the same old problem—clerical confusion, and lack of planning and preparation.

Not until midnight, and they were ready to faint with fatigue, heat and hunger, did they actually learn where they were to spend the remainder of the night. By that time all of them had been fingerprinted, interrogated, their history as humans and suspected aliens again recorded, and each of them assigned an internment number.

But the greatest shock, to the entering internees, was their quarters. Most of them had guessed by now that Poston was being populated before it was even built. Like at Santa Anita, the

REGISTRATION LINE, POSTON RELOCATION CAMP

Notwithstanding the fact that they were registered, interrogated, and medically processed at the "assembly centers," the worried and anxious evacuees were again forced through the lines as they entered the relocation camp at Poston.

—WRA Photo, National Archives.

barrack buildings, of new pine lumber and odorous tarpaper, were finished only as far as framing and roofs. Few windows and doors had been hung, and inside not even a wall partition had been erected. The block captain explained it as "the shortage." Sash, lumber, manpower, were critical. Again the internees must "make do."

"Make do," of course, meant that scores of men, women, and children, must bed down in one large room. The only amelioration to the insufferable heat was the fact that, so far at least, the buildings had gaping holes where windows should be.

But before any sleeping could be done, together or otherwise, each person, or family head, was handed his or her mattress bags, and ordered to go outside and fill them with straw. To escape the bunkhouse bedlam, most of them were glad enough to go out under the lights, and take turns at the pile.

So fathers, mothers, children again queued up—at the straw piles—weary and sick at heart. To the thinking ones it seemed inconceivable that American citizens, in this twentieth century, could be treated with such diabolical neglect, with such crass indifference as to their rights as citizens and humans. It tried one's faith to look out upon the hundreds of evacuees stuffing mattresses in the night, while a million desert gnats and moths dashed themselves to death in the heat and glare of the Army searchlights.

Next morning, after a sleepless five hours on their pallets, some of the worried tenants arose with the dawn. They crept out and around the huddles of sleeping men and women, and their fretting and restless children. To early risers, the big building was a strange world of open-mouthed faces, twisted gray blankets, and denim tick bags aromatic with straw. In their hastily donned and unchanged garb of yesterday, they stepped out the open and unfinished doorway, and down the three wooden steps, to greet their new home in the desert.

Under any other circumstances, the purple mountains to the west, along which somewhere sluggishly meandered the Colorado River, might have been beautiful. But beauty was a moot

THE BUILDING OF POSTON RELOCATION CENTER

A veritable city, in three units, is hastily thrown up on the Colorado River Desert to house 20,000 evacuees from the assembly centers.

—Poston Collection, courtesy University of Arizona Library.

thing when viewed from the confines of an half-finished concentration camp. Not even the mesh-and-barb fences were completed. But Poston didn't really need to be fenced. The snake-ridden lowlands, miles from habitation, were lethal enough. And a machine gun from any one of the towers could quickly account for anyone not choosing to use the sentry gate at the highway. The present camp, vast, chaotic and unfinished as it was, marked only one unit of the Poston complex. Three miles to the south—and three miles beyond that—they were building units two and three of what had been hoped would be a cohesive and operative city, under the honor pattern of American democracy. Internees facing a new home in these other units, would find them just as unfinshed, just as chaotic, and just as utterly repulsive as the camp through which these Santa Anita candidates now walked at dawning.

The one thing that *was* completed, they quickly noted, were the quarters of the supervisory personnel. These, of course, were Anglos. No shortage of lumber for *their* houses. No shortage of window glass, air conditioners, or tree stock. Disgustedly many turned away from the neat row of cottages, where their *hakujin* occupants were probably allowed to sleep late and eat well.

The Californians of the first caravans out of Santa Anita were not the first arrivals at Poston. Seven thousand tenants already were here; lost in the shells of uncompleted blocks of barracks. These internees, mostly farmers out of California's San Joaquin and Imperial Valleys, and from the vast coastal truck gardens, had been steadily moving in for weeks past.

Accepting the complacent role of the vast majority of evacuees, they had cooperated willingly, even though surrender to incarceration meant financial ruin. All of them were full of resentment and protest, but there had been few evasions and hideouts. Where could there be concealment and refuge, when one wore the face of Nippon?

It was already ending in disaster for the few brave souls who dared test the constitutional right of the government to impound its citizens on a racist basis. Gordon Hirabayashi, a Nisei citizen of the Quaker faith, and a senior at the University of Washington, had intentionally and deliberately violated the Japanese curfew law, which militarily demanded that he, along with all his race, remain indoors between 8 p.m. and 6 a.m. He was arrested, and sentenced to three months imprisonment. He appealed the conviction, but his case was to drag itself all the way to the United States Supreme Court before, in 1943, the validity of the military order was unanimously sustained—and Mr. Hirabayashi no.longer had a case.

Fred Toyosaburo Korematsu, a young American citizen, in love with a Caucasian girl, refused to leave his home in San Leandro, California. His intention was to submit to plastic surgery, marry his *hakujin* sweetheart, and hide out for the duration. But the FBI caught up with him. He was convicted in a federal district court for refusing to comply with Civilian Exclusion Order No. 34, and imprisoned. Korematsu, with legal help of the American Civil Liberties Union, was already battling his way to the Supreme Court. But he too was destined to lose. It would be December 18, 1944, before the highest court in the land, in sustaining his conviction, would uphold the constitutionality of the Evacuation. This landmark decision still hangs like a sword over all minorities, and all Americans.[2]

There were other Japanese Americans, out of the cities and farms, courageous enough to fight Evacuation. All of them lost. The great majority who dragged themselves sadly into the assembly centers, and on into the great relocation camps, by surrendering, had saved themselves from endless roughings of police and courts. They were spared the public humiliation which went with being an incorrigible during wartime.

In the construction chaos of Poston it is doubtful that even the seven thousand first arrivals had settled into complacent satisfaction. Not even a time lead and first choice could have dispersed the initial shock and disappointment that so overwhelmed one at

<hr>

[2]For analysis of the legal battles against Evacuation, see Dillon Myer, *Uprooted Americans,* pp. 259-271; Allan R. Bosworth, *America's Concentration Camps,* pp. 224-230.

first sight of this raw and ugly camp. By now they probably knew only where and how to get their meals, the block area of their incarceration, and the allotted space for their straw-stuffed mattresses. They too awaited completion and partitioning of their respective bunkhouses.

Certainly every evacuee brought with him remembrance of a better home—be he a farmer, shopkeeper, or a fisherman out of Terminal Island. "One look, and I knew it was one hell of a substitute," reminisces Mr. K., who even at this late date, insists on remaining anonymous. "I don't think I can ever forget evacuation. Maybe others can. I'm not built that way. I hated Poston the first day I saw it. I hate it now."

THE ARRIVAL AT POSTON
Bus loads of evacuees from California being brought into Poston Relocation
Camp before completion of barracks and facilities.

—Fred Clark Photograph, Poston Collection, University of Arizona Library.

CHAPTER FOUR

SINCE the Japanese expulsion from the West Coast was only one phase of the enormous burden descended upon the nation in its sudden and necessary facing up to the exigencies of war, it still remains a miracle of accomplishment—this removal and resettlement of a vast segment of population. In the building of ten cities in a period of six months, of which Poston was only one, there was bound to be areas of inadequacy and failure in so heady an undertaking. In view of the parallel necessity of housing the greatest army in America's history, the accomplishment becomes a double miracle. But to an hundred thousand Japanese, rooted out of useful and necessary jobs, torn away from homes and security, the everlasting question still is "Why the hell was it necessary?"

Hysterical as was the hour, there was bound to be some conscience and questioning as to the haste and manner in which the evacuation was being conducted. Officially a Congressional Committee, headed by Representative John H. Tolan, of California, and composed of Congressmen John J. Sparkman of Alabama, Laurence F. Arnold of Illinois, Carl T. Curtis of Nebraska, and George H. Bender of Ohio, was set up as a star panel to hear testimony on the Japanese dilemma from every official in contact with the problem. Difficulty was that the voices of fright and urgency had out-shouted those of calmness and reason.

Starting in February of 1942, sessions of the Tolan Committee had been held in Los Angeles, San Francisco, and Washington,

D. C. The fact that 1942 was an election year brought an endless parade of politicians anxious to get themselves on record against anything that resembled the enemy. Politically, the Committee kept itself sensitively attune. California's Attorney General, Earl Warren, at the time a candidate for the office of the governor, had been ambidextrous in his utterances regarding the explosive issue. As attorney general he had formally taken the position:

A substantial portion of the population of California consists of naturalized citizens and citizens born of parents who migrated to this country from foreign lands. They have in the past and do now represent the highest standards of American citizenship. . . . To question that loyalty or place them in a category different from other citizens is not only cruel in its effect upon them but is also disruptive of the national unity which is so essential in these times.[1]

Then, speaking more like a politician seeking office, came his public declaration:

I have come to the conclusion that the Japanese situation as it exists in this state, may well be the Achilles heel of the entire civilian defense effort. Unless something is done it may bring about a repetition of Pearl Harbor.[2]

While the Committee was attentive and cordial to those with political commitments, in actualy taking testimony, it listened well to such patriotic Jap-hating organizations as the American Legion and Native Sons of the Golden West.

It was the San Francisco session which solidified the conclusions of this Congressional Committee. Most significant is that of forty-three actually testifying before the committee, only nine citizens of Japanese ancestry were allowed to speak. Of the forty-seven written statements honored by the congressmen as testimony, only six were of Japanese origin. There is no question but what the committee did labor long and diligently, and that it did honestly endeavor to be fair and dispassionate in its con-

[1]Attorney General's Opinion, No. 1—N.S. 4083, Feb. 7, 1942.
[2]See Morton Grodzins, *Americans Betrayed*, p. 94.

clusions. But the nation was at war. The suspect people were Japanese.

By May of 1942, Congressman Tolan could sum up the findings of his hard working committee: "It has become clear that a curtailment of the rights and privileges of the American-born Japanese citizens of this country will furnish one of the gravest tests of democratic institutions in our history. As with all previous crises in the nation's history, the preservation of liberties will depend upon the degree to which clear vision is applied to momentary difficulties. . . . Unless a clarification is forthcoming, the evacuation of the Japanese population will serve as an incident sufficiently disturbing to lower seriously the morale of vast groups of foreign-born among our people. America is great because she has transcended the difficulties inherent in a situation which finds all races, all nationalities, all colors and all creeds within her borders. This breadth of vision must be applied to the present circumstances.

"This realization in turn must motivate the operations of the War Relocation Authority. . . . The majority of the evacuees to date are American citizens against whom no charge of individual guilt has been lodged. A constructive performance, therefore, on the part of the War Relocation Authority will go far toward fashioning the whole pattern of our policy on racial and minority groups now and in the post-war world. . . ."[3]

Congressman Tolan concluded his report with pertinent recommendations for helping the evacuee through the trauma of resettlement—such mundane suggestions as housing, wages, aiding the war effort through agriculture, technical and professional skills, and respecting his rights and privileges as a citizen. Unfortunately, by the time the Tolan Committee had come up with whatever humane aspects there were in its findings, the direct power of the Army, under General DeWitt, and backed by Presidential edict, was well into completion of the evacuation,

[3]U.S. Congress, House Report No. 2124, 77th Congress, 2nd Session, May 13, 1942.

with little time left to ponder the niceties of how it should be accomplished.

Meanwhile most of Poston's new pine bunkhouses were still without their partitions, and still possessed few creature comforts. But as the internees flooded in by bus from Southern California, and from other California areas by railroad terminus at Parker, sash and doors were frantically hung by the hard-driven carpenters. Amid the vocal confusion of the fast filling camp, the heat, the swirl of dust, and the scream of power saws, the battle for housing went on through these mad and unreal days.

Bunkhouses were monotonously uniform — those apartments lucky enough to have been partitioned off before occupancy being standard twenty by twenty-five feet, with knot-holes through floors and walls. New as they were, the desert winds already had sifted them with dust, and had heaped it incongruously upon floors and into corners. Each person was now being issued an army cot to fit his or her blankets and straw-stuffed mattress. No chairs, no stoves, no closets, no tables, no screens. If the bunkhouse happened to have been partitioned before occupancy, five to eight people would share the apartment. In those quarters not yet divided, it became a vast hive of communal living.

Over the loudspeakers, and from the block bulletin boards, internees were assured that Poston, in line with humane and enlightened supervisoral procedure, would be a center of, and for, the Japanese Americans who would reside there. Dining rooms and kitchens would be staffed and manned by the internees themselves, and all conscripts and volunteers to the various offices and chores would be paid the standard token wages of from eight to sixteen dollars a month.

The same incentives and pay were offered the work gangs who were to construct the permanent buildings—assembly hall, center offices, library, hospital, and theater. These would be built of adobe, the native Spanish building material everywhere about them. Adobe brick-making would be taught to work classes already started.

Insofar as possible, Poston would be governed by the internees, with officers of their own choosing. A temporary Community Council would be immediately set up, composed of representatives from each block. Voting would be "by all persons in the Center eligible for the Work Corps." Stipulation was "Only American citizens, 21 or older, to be candidates for office," which automatically sidelined the Japan-born Isseis. "Election by majority vote of the block." The function of the Council would be "the making of recommendations to the Project Director on internal affairs, and the establishment of a judicial committee to deal with problems of law and order."[4] Mr. Wade Head was Poston's Project Director.

Each block had its own mess hall, communal recreation center, and laundry facilities. The first meal served the initial Santa Anita inductees in the block's mess hall convinced many of them that the authorities had somehow gotten their work gangs mixed. Pickled beets and boiled rice were ladled out at breakfast, and repeated at noon. The waiting lines were long, the tables noisy and crowded. And the unfinished and as yet glassless hall was almost physically intolerable with its desert heat, dust, and flies. As for the block's still bare and unfinished amusement hall—the internees could draw little amusement from it.

Day after day, as evening approached, they watched the same drama enacted — bus after bus, from Southern California or Parker, dusty with the miles, entering through the gates, spewing out the loads of weary and bewildered humanity. Internees with clerical experience quickly volunteered themselves to the processing center, doing all in their power to aid the depressed, frightened and sometimes embittered families to find places in the community.

All day long one listened to the scream of power saws and the thump of hammers as the construction race went on to provide housing for those displaced people ahead of the pace with which the government displaced them.

[4]These provisions set up by the WRA for temporary government seem to have been fairly uniform in all Relocation Centers.

77]

PARKER, ARIZONA, 1942

Photograph taken at the approximate time Poston Relocation Camp was built.
Parker was the railroad terminus, approximately sixteen miles north of Poston I.
The town is on the east bank of the Colorado River.

In their previous map-scanning, few had ever been conscious of the land area where Poston was rising. It could have been the Valley of the Moon, for all they had known about it. Now their learning processes were painfully quickening.

Poston, they soon discovered, was located on Indian land, a sort of lost world between Wickenburg and Needles—and one of the hottest spots imaginable. Actually it was Indian reservation, housing twelve hundred Mojaves and Chemehuevis, and therefore technically under the thumb of the Honorable John Collier and his Bureau of Indian Affairs. Many internees, wise enough to understand, were alarmed with the thought that Japanese Americans were now slotted in with the Indians on a tribal reservation. Knowing the Indian Bureau's dismal record in handling the welfare of their aboriginal charges, they had reason to be doubly worried.

But if Poston was emerging as Japanese-Indian reservation, it was flowering badly even for the Indian Bureau. Most Indian reservations were the abode of a racial minority, defrauded, neglected and oppressed. But so far their portals were not guarded by machine guns and soldiery, nor were they encircled by mesh and barbed wire. And already Parker Valley had its Indian population outnumbered ten to one by this frantic in-thrust of Orientals.

Nearest town was Parker, Arizona—seventeen miles north, through sagebrush, mesquite, and creosote brush. Parker, edging the east bank of the Colorado, was a stop on the Santa Fe Railroad, and feverish construction base for the giant Parker Dam rising farther upstream, and now the equally feverish supply terminus for the great three-unit wartime city rising southward. In point of population, the Mojaves and Chemehuevis were already lost numerically.

One had to grudge that the WRA, charged by governmental decree with the dramatic and overwhelming task of the relocation, was striving as best it could to keep the thing within the framework of democratic ideals. Internees were reminded that Charles Poston, whose name graced the Parker Valley segment of the ten great camps the WRA was building throughout the west, was one of the pioneer fathers of Arizona—revered and remembered. Poston as a government engineer, had visioned Parker Valley, as early as 1864, as filled with settlers, and green with crops. He had drafted an irrigation system to accomplish it—but somehow this desert blossoming had never become a reality.

But now, with the newly-created Parker Dam and its giant canals, it was believed that Poston's dream was to become a living thing. Eighty thousand acres of arid land would now green out in beauty and usefulness. The ambitious and productive Japanese—world's finest farmers—would accomplish this miracle. So long as the war lasted—probably long after—here would be their city—here would be their home.

Their neighboring communities, aside from the former mining town of Parker, was Blythe to the south, with its desert-trained soldiery. From this camp, Poston drew its guards. On the river, farther south, was Yuma City. A mile below Parker could be found Silver City, a pretty little government town, with lawns, trees, and air-conditioned housing. Silver City was Indian Agency headquarters. There, in comfort, lived the bureaucrats who not only ran the Indian affairs, but Poston Relocation Camp as well.

Unit One of Poston, of which the initiates from Santa Anita were a part, was located on a cleared area of several square miles. Its blocks of wood-and-tarpaper barracks had been erected, or were in speedy process. Each block—or *buraku* as the inmates already had named them—contained a dozen or more of these bunkhouses, temporary recreation hall, mess hall, latrines, and a laundry and ironing room. The washing machines were yet to be provided.

Mr. John Evans, Chief Administrative Officer, was a young man of thirty-seven years, who, with his family, lived at the Indian Agency headquarters. He had been with the Indian Service since his graduation from high school. He had entered it as a timekeeper, and, after taking courses at the American University, in Washington, D. C., and at the Alexander Hamilton Institute had, prior to Poston, become a senior accountant and auditor for the Service. His clothes were neatly tailored in western style, and he wore expensive high-heeled boots.[5]

Mr. Wade Head, Chief Project Officer, was a fifty-year-old man from Texas. His education was more practical than academic, though he did possess training in engineering and business. He had formerly worked for the Indian Service, but for the six years prior to Poston, he had served as a Deputy U. S. Marshal, in Tucson. He had come back into the Indian Service to step in as Operations Chief of Poston. He likewise lived away from the project, and graced it with his presence only when he had to.[6]

Though honest, and inflexible, Head apparently had little sympathy with the Japanese. If they were not enemies, they were racial products of the enemy. It was everywhere alleged that he considered them inferior, deceitful, and never to be trusted. They were the people his nation was fighting. Handle them justly, but firmly. That was his policy.

Nell Findley, the only female on the staff, was Chief of Community Services.

Now the internees began to meet more of their Anglo bosses and associates. Some of these *hakujins* were good, some were inept. Some had, because of wartime scarcity and opportunity, stepped into lucrative jobs, with little experience or capability. Others, sensing the heartbreak of the evacuation, were deeply sympathetic toward their charges, and dedicated and hardworking in their efforts to make Poston workable and habitable. Good or bad, one had to accept them. There was no choice.

The only really completed projects were the water towers, and the sewage disposal system. Canals, under construction, from Parker Dam, would irrigate the acreage on which the prisoners would be expected to grow their own foodstuffs, and nurture the gayule plants which the government was hauling in from

[5]See Alexander H. Leighton, *The Governing of Men*, p. 87.
[6]*Ibid.*, p. 88.

Mexico. Sap from the gayule, it was hoped, would ease the nation's already acute rubber shortage.

On a clear day, when the dust storms were not blowing, one could see the two other units of Poston under construction. Unlike the huge honor city most internees had envisioned, each would be run as a separate community. Like the nine other immense camps in the western states, Poston was generally under direction of the War Relocation Authority, headed by Milton Eisenhower, though Poston was complicated by a duality control of the Indian Bureau, since it stood on Indian lands. John Collier was Washington's Commissioner of Indian Affairs, and, since Poston's top managers lived at Silver City or Parker, and authority and direction came out of the Indian Bureau office, the WRA appeared to be only incidental to its management.

But the Indian Service began the task most hopefully—as the first mimeographed directives clearly indicated. Quickly as possible, Poston was to become economically self-sufficient. In time of war, with every dollar and all manpower in demand, it was important to convert the Center from an item of government expense into an asset. By this means, the directives hopefully pointed, personnel, material and money would be released for other work, and thousands of idle Japanese would become busy in agriculture and certain kinds of manufacturing needed for the war effort. But it was late; fall was approaching. The canals must yet be finished, the camp was still too chaotic for manufactury. The great hopes were not likely to materialize before 1942 closed itself out.

In spite of the high sounding resolutions and reminders, most of the internees were of the opinion that the war effort could have been better served had they been allowed to remain at home and aid America with the skills for which they were trained. As farmers on the Pacific slope, they could have produced vast crops of the foodstuffs now so desperately needed in wartime America. They were immensely competent fishermen, business operators, and intelligent and willing workers. At Poston, as in the assembly centers, the young Niseis repeatedly begged for their citizens' share in the military. Here they were, in the Arizona desert—idle, denied, and most generally useless. And to house and incarcerate them, millions of dollars were being wasted in lumber, building materials, and manpower—all critically needed elsewhere.

Supervisors of the burgeoning camp had no reliable or direct way of knowing what the stress of crowding and lack of privacy were doing to the family units of the *nihonjin* population. Family structure to Asiatics was, and always had been, the key center of life. Pressure, humiliation and inchoate anger were bringing a turmoil of wit and wills unknown to the compact communities of Fish Harpor or the Little Tokyos of California's cities. Surface view across the great spread of Poston's barracks could never indicate the growing cleavage between Issei and Nisei, the extent to which the oldsters had turned thoughts back to peaceful remembrance of their racial past, nor the separation of the American-born young men into cliques of bitterness.

Neither the Indian Bureau, the War Relocation Authority, nor Management seemed to show any glimmer of understanding of the acute needs and problems of the thousands upon thousands of internees swelling the population. Mr. K., remembering his Poston incarceration, tells it thus: "Somehow the second generation seemed rude in the eyes of their parents. Language difficulty probably accounted for a lot of it. But there were other things, too. We no longer understood one another—parents and children, that is. We couldn't talk things over. In the Center it was far worse than before the evacuation. Before that lousy heave-ho, parents and children, eating together, would discuss family matters. But in Poston, it couldn't be done. We didn't see each other often enough, and we stopped eating together as families. Young folks associated with young folks. Older people had only themselves for company. The Center only aggravated Issei resentment of the way the Nisei took over, and tried to run things."

Mr. Eisenhower and Mr. Collier were, of course, far removed from the camps they supposedly were directing. But the swaggering Texans and cowboys who were running this strange show, seemed basically just as far removed, when it came to awareness or comprehension of even the simplest needs of their charges.

Many an internee could have told them that the first grave governmental mistake, aside from the injustice of the evacuation itself, was the lumping together of all *nihonjin,* under the supposition that all were as alike in thought as they were in skin and facial features. Even at Santa Anita this great cleavage had been at work. The Isseis, born in Japan, moved like automats under the Old World culture and patterns. Many of them were unable to cope with English, and others talked the language only with difficulty. With the ban on all Japanese language publications, they had become islands of isolation, neglect, and suspicion. Long before there was a war, these people had witnessed the splitting from them of their flesh and blood by the harsh, new, incomprehensible culture of America.

In this land the young folks were openly contemptuous of *bushido,* or the traditional ideals of personal conduct; of *baishaku* arrangements in marriage, where the honored parents chose mates for their children, with the elaborate system of "go-betweens" for the principal families. Emperor worship, father honor and respect, family rituals and ceremonies, all were passed airily along, or scoffed at. As to the Issei custom of *ojigi* bowings between friends and peers, most Niseis considered this as strictly for the birds. Even *jicho,* the *nihonjin* pattern of self-respect, was in danger of losing its meaning. In America, things were indeed different.

So, at Poston, as at Santa Anita, Isseis were lonely and aloof. Stung by segregation, sidelined by contempt and neglect, they grew ever more stubborn and uncooperative.

The Kibeis, American-born citizens, but whose parents had sent them back to Japan for at least a part of their schooling, were apt to be considerably more culturally tied to the Old Country ways and outlook, but extremely emancipated because of their free-wheeling American days. Many considered themselves citizens of both countries. The duality of their loyalties kept them more or less aloof from and uncomfortable in the circles of both Isseis and Niseis. The cultural cleavage going on in the camps made them suspect to both sides. They were rapidly becoming clannish problem children among the internees.

Niseis, on the other hand, born in America, educated in America, and as American in outlook and concept as any child of Oklahoma or New York, already had gone their separate ways from the old folks and Kibeis in everything from food to language and manners. Not for them the bowings and scrapings, the Papa worship, the endless ceremonies. To them there was no remembrance of a divine emperor, and they were apt to laugh aloud at any suggestion of *baishaku* go-between, or parental selection or meddling in marriage.

Niseis and Isseis were as boldly separated in culture as the Greeks and the Eskimos. If the hoped-for self-government of Poston, so constantly prated over the loudspeakers, and so consistently reminded in the mimeographed sheets on the block bulletin boards, ever was to become a reality, some WRA minds needed quickly to come to grips with the facts.

Many an Issei dreamed fondly of the mother country left so many years ago. Some of them stubbornly clung to belief in the divinity of the emperor. Some of them, because of recent hurts, had become disillusioned with American justice and democracy. Actually there were a few who believed and hoped Japan would win the war. But, for the most part, Isseis stood as a group, misunderstood, neglected, frightened, bewildered, and passed over as potential leaders in Poston's vast, raw community.

To an indifferent, hostile management, the Niseis were even less inclined to unburden. There was no one among the *hakujin* bosses to whom one could resolutely or comfortably talk out the fears. For, if anything, Niseis were far more hurt and embittered by the uprooting and discrimination. It was impossible not to resent the manner in which their rights in American citizenry had been trampled and betrayed.

At Santa Anita committee after committee of Niseis had offered to join their American comrades in Army and Navy enlistments, war bond drives—anything to prove their love and loyalty to the nation of their birth. At Terminal Island, at Japanese communities everywhere, many a Nisei young man had been classified as 1-A, and eligible for draft or enlistment. Before Pearl Harbor, hundreds of Japanese Americans had actually been called up for duty. But then came the hysteria, and the hectic "assembly center" period, and most of the eligible male Niseis suddeny found themselves reclassified as 4-C. To willing Niseis, that was another name for poison. These things were being remembered at Poston.

No one, not even the *hakujin* supervisors, seemed to comprehend that Niseis were American citizens; that they too had hate for the common enemy; that they were as quick to reject the thought of Japanese victory as any other American. It was a weird half-world they now lived in.

Through the scorching heat of summer days, through the choking, swirling dust of the "Poston zephyrs," there were gripe sessions and plenty of talk. One had only to walk into the recreation halls, the camp stores, or listen to the vocal rumble in the barracks, to know what the supervisors could not or would not see. Superficially, self-government was being worked out. Underneath, the great camp already had divided itself into factions and fraternities.

There were clandestine circles of every shade and leaning. There were the militant and angry Niseis meeting in bunkhouse gangs, and at the Judo Club. The more Japan-oriented and jingoistic of the Kibeis were busy in their secretive and aloof talk sessions. Isseis moved in their own world of tradition and thought.

There were opportunists who dealt in whiskey, cigarettes, black market chocolate, sugar, nylons, and rare items unavailable at the Poston stores. Nefarious peddlers, by special collusion with the supply-truck drivers in and out of camp, and Caucasian visitors, were able to make profit out of want and misery. On a food allotment of less than forty cents a day, there was little to hoard and peddle from what could be garnered out of the mess halls—

[86

but poverty forced many to barter this last pitiful resource for gain.

And through it all there was one conspirational necessity—the stealing of lumber and plywood for the apartment partitions which the Army, War Relocation Authority and Management had utterly failed to provide. Poston, vast and chaotic, stood divided in thought, darkly secretive, desperate in necessity, and, in many ways, a dozen worlds apart.

CHAPTER FIVE

IN WASHINGTON some official minds *must* have been at work trying to unravel the complexities of evacuation, or at least to have some awareness of the physical and psychological shock which the internment camps had brought upon the evacuees— though as the Arizona summer burned itself out to fall, one could see no discernible evidence of any such compassion or understanding trickling down to the frame and tarpaper world of Poston. In the lower echelon of management, Mr. Wade Head, Mr. John Evans, and their assistants, were competent, hardboiled administrators. But to them, apparently, a Jap was a Jap; with no particular shade of difference.

The ten great camps of the Relocation Authority were now operative, and had settled down to a peculiar sort of permanence. Poston was by far the largest. But all of them were fair-sized cities. Besides Poston, with a population of 20,000, Arizona had another camp, at Gila River, with another 15,000 internees— the pair being third and fourth largest cities in the state. In California there was Manzanar, with a capacity of 10,000; and Tule Lake, built with an expectation of housing up to 16,000 recalcitrants. Minidoka, Idaho, with a capacity of 10,000; Heart Mountain, Wyoming, housing 10,000; Granada, Colorado, with 8,000; Topaz, Utah, with 10,000; and Arkansas had two camps, one at Rohwer, with 10,000; one at Jerome, with 10,000.[1]

[1]See Allan R. Bosworth, *America's Concentration Camps*, p. 120.

The first big push at Poston was the War Relocation Work Corps. Every internee—resident, or new arrival—was expected to sign themselves into the grand concept of complacency, compliance, and busy hands. Most of them scribbled their names to the mimeographed document with the same ennui they signed everything else; many without even reading it. Only a few of the hard core and embittered aliens refused to accept this or any other pledge.

I swear loyalty to the United States and enlist in the War Relocation Work Corps for the duration of the war and fourteen days thereafter in order to contribute to the needs of the nation and in order to earn a livelihood for myself and my dependents. I will accept whatever pay the War Relocation Authority determines, and I will observe all the rules and regulations.

In doing this I understand that I shall not be entitled to any cash or allowance beyond the wages due me at the time of discharge from the Work Corps; that I may be transferred from one relocation center to another by the War Relocation Authority; that medical care will be provided, but that I cannot make a claim against the United States for any injury or disease acquired by me while in the Work Corps; that I shall be subject to special assessments for educational, medical and other community services as may be provided for in the support of any dependents who reside in a relocation center; that I shall be financially responsible for the full value of any government property that I use whie in the Work Corps; and that the infraction of any regulations of the War Relocation Authority will render me liable to trial and suitable punishment. So help me God.[2]

Because the internees unhesitatingly signed the WRA pledge, walked circumspectly, and rebelled none at the rules, no matter how strange or shattering, the Chief Administrative Officer, the Chief Fiscal Officer, and their supervisors, eyed the great camp in their charge as a good camp—filled with compliant, peaceful, adaptive humans.

"I signed the Work Corps pledge without bothering to read it, or even caring what it said," remembers Nobu Shimahara. "What choice did one have? People just lined up and signed."

[2]As quoted and summarized in Leighton, Alexander H., *The Governing of Men*, pp. 64-65.

Today Nobu Shimahara is superintendent of one of the largest bookbinding firms in Los Angeles. He smiles a little wryly as he recalls his time at Poston. "I was eighteen years old when my family landed there. From the time we were ordered out of Los Angeles, we'd had dozens of papers shoved at us. Who cared? One just signed. I needed a job in Poston. My name on the Work Corps pledge got me the job.

"Oddy, my job was in the Camp's sign department. There I discovered I was a fair hand at lettering. I liked making signs— even at eight dollars a month. I was a sign maker most of the time I stayed at Poston.

"The only thing that bothered me, when the government handed over these official papers demanding this and ordering that, was that no one ever thought or cared to ask, 'Are you an American citizen?' That was the thing that really got to you."

At Poston, as at other camps, a special corps of community analysts, educated and degree-holding anthropologists and sociologists, were being added to view and advise on the adaptive problems of the internees. Around this Anglo staff of administrators and experts were the silent, willing Nisei clerks, typists and workers, laboring at pittance wages. To management in general, all was well.

But the promised partitions for the barracks had not yet arrived. If one wanted sleeping privacy for his family, he was forced to jeopardize his record as a complacent internee by stealing lumber and plywood, as so many had done. The token wage promised for daily labor had not been covered by a single check from WRA. Internees were in desperate need of things from the Poston store.

The mutterings from the work gangs—on the canals—at the adobe brick project—the farming—the camp construction—was, by now, loud enough for even the community analysts to hear.

Fall had brought surcease from the enervating heat and dust of summer, but the hospital, still housed in its tarpapered barrack, had remained as makeshift as ever. Its *hakujin* director, Dr. Abraham Pressman, was still valiantly battling with the

WETTING DOWN THE DESERT EARTH
The only possible way to hold the Arizona soil during a "Poston zephyr."
–*Poston Collection, courtesy University of Arizona Library.*

WRA for improvements and better quarters — but rehousing, equipment, drugs, and supplies were as slow coming as the promised pay.

Dysentery—the amoebic kind that somehow had crept from Mexico's near border into Poston—and probably abetted by the poor quality and badly cooked food—was epidemic. Measles, influenza, and the mysterious lung congestion of the desert, already endemic in the Army's desert camps, had set their claws upon the internees. Tuberculosis was on the rise. The crude, inadequate hospital was stuffed to overflowing.

Ominous as were the portents at Poston, there still were a number of good signs. But these gains were not initiated by the WRA or the Indian Bureau. They sprang up as basic needs, and flowered out of the spiritual hunger and soul-deep necessity of a complex culture under stress.

Protestants and Catholics held Sunday worship in the block centers, with both Christian Isseis and Niseis for audience. The Methodist minister, a thirty-seven-year-old Issei who spoke both English and Japanese fluently, had headed churches in Mesa, Arizona and Bakersfield, California. He had conducted one of the first Christian services in Poston, and had drawn fire from management and Buddhists alike for his outspoken and energetic efforts in behalf of Christian *nihonjins* whose rights were being trampled in the suppressive ferment of the evacuation. He was an enthusiastic participants in the Civic Planning Board, and helped draw up the camp's first constitution. This document named the rights of the evacuees, gave voting privileges to all camp residents over the age of twenty-one, and guaranteed that the Self-Government Council would be composed of representatives from every block, to hear and act on grievances concerning the camp and its conduct.

Out of sheer boredom on Sundays there was heavy participation in the Christian services. Each of the camp's three units boasted from three to ten Protestant Ministers, and one or two Catholic Fathers. Many internees visited all sects in rotation. Sunday worship in Poston was a live and moving thing. But it was establishment of a Buddhist temple, in the fall, that truly pleased the multitude.

The affair was spontaneous, but once started, it moved fast. The Isseis especially took this project to heart, and there was never a lack of willing hands to erect the fragile and beautiful little structure in record time. Isseis, steeped in the faith, and Kibeis, exposed to it in the Mother Country, forgot bitterness and aloofness long enough to strain muscles, and sweat along with the other internees, until the bright-colored temple with its shrine and classrooms shone like a red and yellow jewel amid the raw pine and tarpaper world of Poston.

Naturally there was uneasiness in the upper echelons of management about the Buddhist upsurge. Some of the Anglo-Christian bosses openly labeled it "paganism." The anthropologists and sociologists of the community analysis corps looked down their *hakujin* noses at it, just as they did at any other form of divine worship. But for once they were wise enough to keep hands off the project, and did not interfere.

But like the Christians, the Buddhists were hopelessly splintered as to sects and formality of worship—the Shin Shu, the Odaishi, and the Micheron, all quarreling for rights. Out of the dispute came a composite worship for all three, with the Shin Shu ritual having a slight predominance. Soon there was a second temple at Poston, and a temple each for Units II and III.[3] But most important, cooperation and tolerance had worked. The predominant religion of the Japanese people was allowed to function. Once again was heard the Sutras and Senryus recited on the Sabbath. The internees knew how good this was for Poston.

With fall, too, had come the schools, and their establishment. The classes, in their crude huts, had gotten off to an unpromising start, and the permanent school structure, being built by camp low-pay labor, was not yet completed. The usually bright

[3]For detailed study of Buddhism at Poston, see "Poston Community Analysis Report No. 14;" and "Buddhist Organization," by Bussei Leader, George Yamaguchi. Poston Collection, University of Arizona Library.

youngsters, yanked out of California's superb classrooms and shoved into tarpapered shacks amid the unreality, dust, and bugs of Poston, were responding poorly. Puzzling attitude and deportment had become genuine problems.

In the summer, Dr. Miles E. Cary, a Caucasian educator from Hawaii, and former principal of Honolulu's McKinley High School, was appointed as Poston's Director of Education. To handle the 5,000 students who answered the call, seventy-five Nisei evacuees had been given crash courses in education in the hope of aiding the camp's qualified teaching personnel in handling Poston's classrooms for the fall and winter term. The Department of Adult Education was handed over to the guidance of Dr. John Powell, staff head of Community Activities.

A member of the National Student Relocation Council paid visit to the Center. Some of the camp's college students, through the Council's efforts, were able to resume their education in eastern colleges and universities, out of the "hate belt" of the Far West.[4] Farsighted as were these efforts, they came too late to help many thousands of bewildered youngsters enrolling for the first time in the three units of Poston.

There was constant criticism of the school program by the parents who watched, disturbed by the downgrading of education brought on by the whole stupid evacuation program. They wanted facilities and teaching like they had known in California. They wanted teachers of ability and experience, not half-educated Niseis, themselves scarcely out of school, and hustled through a few summer training-lectures.

Dr. Cary, as Director of Education, found himself in an unconscionable squeeze. Shortages of trained personnel, inadequate facilities, and inability of the WRA to increase its financial and physical aid, became a trying experience for this dedicated man. Bravely he appealed to the people:

What do you want our Poston schools to do for you and with your children? Your answer to this question would reveal the kind of

[4]See Leighton, *The Governing of Men*, p. 101.

world you desire when this war is over. It would reveal too, the stand you are taking in the present world civil war.

I believe that most of you want your boys and girls to be helped to live rich, significant lives in America. I believe, too, you want them helped to learn how to have a part to share in building the better world of the future.

What would a better world be like? A world in which a man, regardless of pigmentation, would be treated with respect. A world in which each individual, according to his powers, would be encouraged to make his special contributions toward improving the common life.

Insofar as I am able, I shall encourage our teachers to work along the lines suggested above. I hope you approve.[5]

Concerned as he was, Dr. Cary failed to get the full approval and cooperation he so desperately sought. Even the adobe school buildings, still far from finished, were looked upon with worry and suspicion. Tarpapered shacks were bad enough, but mud schools, to the *nihonjin* mind, were unfamiliar, inferior, and degrading. To work at adobe making ruined the internees' clothes, which the government would not replace. Wages of eight to twelve dollars a month were not enough for the labor and the loss, and the *hakujin* foreman, hired at high pay, was hard, bossy, and looked down his Anglo nose at the bitter and angry little men who slaved at his command.

There were whispers that the buildings, when completed, would be for the Indians, rather than the Japanese, or were planned as hospitals for wounded soldiers. The whole plan, it was rumored, was to get a lot of work for next to nothing. Progress lagged, and the children, despite every protest, attended their classes in makeshift quarters, with whatever teaching staff Dr. Cary could find at hand.[6]

The first death had occurred fifteen days after the first evacuees had entered the half-finished camp—that was May 23. The following day a simple service was held in the dusty and barren

[5]*Poston Notes and Activities,* magazine, Henry Mori, editor. Issue I.
[6]See Leighton, *The Governing of Men,* pp. 104-105.

camp. "The planning and execution of a funeral in the early days was made difficult by limited facilities; the people were not prepared to face the situation. When everyone was filled with bitterness and antipathy toward evacuation, the first funeral did not help to elevate the people's morale. They were trying to get accustomed to the new and strange environment."[7]

By August the procedures for handling the dead were at least partially organized. Poston, by now, had practically reached population capacity. But funerals, Christian or Buddhist, still had to be hasty affairs—within twenty-four hours of bereavement. The body was prepared in one corner of the shack-housed hospital, with only a bed-screen shutting off the macabre operation from the live patients in the room. After the speedy funeral, Buddhist, Shinto or Christian, the cadaver was shipped to Yuma, and then on to San Diego for cremation.

An enterprising undertaker from Yuma became low bidder to the WRA for all mortuary work at Poston, and as the three great camps filled to capacity, quantity alone made it profitable. As a move toward efficiency, the firm set up shop in camp. In the heat of the summer months, in that traumatic year of 1942, the alert and adaptive undertaker commenced erection of a crematory alongside the hospital, where it would be handy. The concrete foundation for this building was laid before the internees discovered the intent and purpose of the new structure. Through their elected Community Council, they began to raise stormy hell.

"The issue was brought to light, and it caused heated arguments throughout the appointed personnel, Council, Block Managers, and in block meetings. Evacuees thought that a crematory annexed to the hospital would create a demoralizing effect on the patients. There were other ways of reasoning, but the morale viewpoint was the main line of attack. . . . After much discussion, the project reimbursed the contractor for the construction. A new site was chosen in the warehouse area; the crematory was

[7]Report No. 79, "Funerals in Poston," Paul Higashi. Poston Collection, University of Arizona Library.

THE HOSPITAL

The hospital at Poston I, always chronically inadequate, was later housed in

completed in October, 1942, to the satisfaction of the residents.'[8] With disposal of the corpses now conveniently arranged, camp funerals became more leisurely and more elaborate affairs. In California, Japanese funerals had been noted for their colorful profusion of flowers. In the desert dust of Parker Valley this live and fragrant feature had to be modified to fit the time and place. But in creative skills the *nihonjins* were never lacking. Flowers began to show again in the funerals held in the block recreation halls. But the flowers—bright and beautiful though they were— were entirely artificial. Colored paper, and skilled and artistic hands, had filled the lack.

Death, wherever it happens, is tragic. But death in the sprawling and ugly concentration camps of World War II was a shattering experience to any family so hit. In California, the law required that ashes of the deceased must permanently repose in a mausoleum, cemetery, or church vault. The Buddhist temples of California, or the family burial grounds of Mother Japan, had received much of the human ashes prior to Pearl Harbor. Now, indeed, it was different.

The State of Arizona, on the other hand, was more liberal. It permitted families to keep their urns at home. In the case of Poston, home meant the family section of a *buraku*. The best the WRA could furnish for cremated remains was a paper carton.[9] Poston's enterprising mortician could supply the needed urn, provided the internee had come through the Japanese roust with enough money to pay for it. But, whether in paper carton, or ornate receptacle, the ashes of the loved ones sat with the *butsuden* altar and death tablets in many a family circle of Poston's barracks.

The stress, problems and heartaches seemed almost more than the internee could bear—this first and ugly year of 1942. But bear it they did. On the plus side were indications the government at last had reached conviction that all Japanese Americans were not inscrutable villains. There was talk now that enlist-

[8]*Ibid.,* p. 2.
[9]*Ibid.,* p. 4.

ments into military service were soon to be made available to the camp's young men. Schools at Poston, confusedly and haltingly commenced, now moved along lethargically. And the internees were settling down to the almost hopeless monotony of their imprisonment.

The adobe walls of the permanent structures had begun to rise, despite resistance and alarm, and would include administration offices, theater, assembly hall, and the desperately needed hospital. Construction had started on the big fence. The main canal, from Parker Dam, so necessary for the farming operations, was getting its first water. Enterprising young Niseis had diverted part of the stream directly into Poston I. It flowed into camp from the east, midway between blocks 16 and 17, west past the adobe school project, and was diverted south past the drygoods store and shoe repair shop. Along its route, the young men had scooped out three huge basins in the earth. When filled with canal water, they became Poston's swimming pools.

There was, however, a feature about these aquatic diversions unique to Poston. The pools seemed to draw almost as many rattlesnakes from the desert terrain as they did swimmers from the internees. As a safety measure, the surrounding scrub brush was cleared away. But even then, daily, the sidewinders and the king-size Arizona diamondbacks had to be ladled from the pools in order to keep them even moderately safe for the enjoyment of the swimmers.

Even as the camp grew seemingly endless in size, it settled down into a crazy-quilt pattern of religious and social life. A volunteer fire department had been organized to cope with the sudden blazes in the flimsy structures and the more constant hazard of greater conflagrations. Its police force was staffed with *nihonjins*. Police Chief Kiyoshi Shigekawa headed the main force at Unit I. Harry Madokoro and Ken Sato served as Chiefs at Units II and III. The big jail was at Unit I, and had a moderate use for those overcome with the whiskey bootlegged into camp, the gamblers who grew obstreperous enough to draw knives, or turn to the muscle mayhem of *judo* and *karate* when things fared badly at the camp's constant gaming at dice, cards and *go* boards. The jail too housed its share of political and factional warriors, and those participants in neighborly brawls occasioned by too close confinement.

On the comfort side, many internees had scooped the earth out from under their barracks. These cellars, if one felt inclined to brave the hazard of migrating scorpions and snakes, were cooling spots for the more ambitious of Poston's citizens.

Dance bands had been recruited among the Nisei musicians and, Saturday nights the throb of music could be heard in many a block recreation hall. The Isseis, a little contemptuous of the brash and noisy younger set, clung to their Buddhist associations, Shinto and tea societies. They had even set themselves up an old-world bath house to show their utter abhorrence of the unrestful atmosphere of the public showers alongside their multiple-holed latrines. There were a number of shamisen musicians in camp, and many an Issei was adept at the contemplative and meaningful tea ceremonies. The native ways, at least to some, were still important.

An inquiring mind could have discerned many plus developments at Poston. But even the most encouraging progress was overshadowed by the darker specter of unrest and erosion. To Poston's citizenry, what was unseen was a fearsome thing. Yet to camp management, and apparently to Mr. Eisenhower and Mr. Collier in Washington, all was calm, and all was quiet.

SEWING SCHOOL, POSTON CENTER
One of a number of projects instituted for the benefit of the internees.

CHAPTER SIX

MINISCULE as were the wages paid Poston's internees, even that was chronically in arrears. In October, many of them had not been paid since July. Ninety days had again passed since the last slender pay check had been tendered hundreds of the Work Corps whose hands made the adobes, lifted the walls, dug the canals, plowed the desert earth, or manned the offices and dining halls. Added to the misery caused by loss of livelihood, and the still impounded bank accounts of many internees, there was genuine want in the colony. Tiny as were the wages, the money was essential. There was a desperate need.

To many an unpaid worker, it was particularly aggravating to know that the *hakujin* personnel received their fat salary checks regularly, for the identical work done side-by-side with the internees at only a fraction of the pay scale. For a lot of internees, not even that fraction was being paid.

Hope had been raised that great forces of residents were to be released from Poston to harvest cotton in the southern Arizona and California's Imperial Valley fields. Pay would be the prevailing wage, driven to all-time high by labor scarcity. The Poston administration had made much of this opportunity, and a thousand applicants had begged for the work. But the administration was stopped cold by a military order forbidding release of internees to the project. The Western Defense Command wanted no "Japs" loosed in or near strategic areas. Again the people felt they had been betrayed. Again they lost heart.

Then came news that a camouflage-net factory, much larger than the one at Santa Anita, was to be established at Poston. The factory, however, was to be set up and operated by private interests. It would use internees, but at the prison wage. The pay phase came like a slap in the face to this proud people. The firm, it was felt, would reap solid profits in selling their product to the government. Its operation would add nothing to the welfare of Poston as a community. The projected enterprise was viewed as crass exploitation of a needy people already reduced to servitude.

When the raw material for the nets began arriving in Poston, many of the men utterly refused to unload it. The administration leveled the accusation of "sabotage." The internees answered by calling it "exploitation." Those who remembered Santa Anita were glad to be free even of the specter of again weaving colored burlap into chicken wire.

Some of the people were literally in rags. They had been herded into camp with only the barest personal belongings allowed, especially in clothes and creature comforts. At Santa Anita, and the other assembly centers, a few dollars a month had been issued as clothing allowance. At Poston, similar promises had been made—but, like everything else, delivery on promise was just as chronically in arrears.

Every move of the WRA seemed to be laden with confusion, mismanagement, and vacillation. The internees, rubbed raw by an hundred injustices, were sensitive, and growing daily more suspicious of administrative intent and purpose. For one thing, evacuation's great gathering had commenced only months after Pearl Harbor. Herded like animals into camps, the internees had been and were now completely out of touch with the great American world they once had known.

They had no way of knowing that much of the deprivations they were suffering was a common lot with the rest of the nation. The camp hotheads, justified as they were in their vociferous protests, were unwittingly contrasting the plight of the *nihonjin* with a fat and prosperous America they had known before the war—not with an America terribly deprived and shackled by the demands of an all-out and world-wide struggle.

The degree-holding community analysts, staffed in all the camps to study this human stress, were alarmed by the hate and lack of understanding they were witnessing in management. They were equally concerned with the unrealistic thinking of many of the internees, now suddenly dominated by the aroused old men among the Isseis, and prodded by some of the Japan-educated Kibeis.

What was most desperately needed was liaison and understanding between management and people. "Fiscal Office was what you call racist in attitude," says Mr. K. "It took a snotty pose toward internees. High as God Almighty. Its bosses didn't like Japs, and we didn't like them. We didn't dare trust the bosses, and we didn't trust that circus of young college egg heads that worked with them. They seemed to be in kind of a silent daze. Who knew what side they were on? The only voice we had was the camp newspaper. And everyone knew the censors were boring down on that."

The camp publication had started as the *Press-Bulletin*, to eventually emerge as the *Poston Chronicle*. Its pattern of emergence varied, from weekly, semi-weekly, to daily, and, eventually, back again—probably dictated by wartime paper scarcity, inclination and emotion of its editors, and the barometrical pressure of Poston's populace. It possessed none of the freedom and swing of the long-suppressed language sheets, and everyone knew it was management-dominated. As could be expected, it was turned out of duplicating machines instead of being neatly printed. But with all its faults, the *Chronicle* was a good thing for Poston.

Hundreds of the workers, angered at what they considered betrayal, no longer showed up at the daily task. Work stoppage was something even Fiscal Management was not too blind to recognize. Directives against the malcontents were posted on the block bulletin boards. The Project Director stormed at and threatened a group of the Community Council who called on him with their grievances. The FBI joined the community

BEGINNING OF NEWSPAPERING AT POSTON

The *Press-Bulletin,* started with one typewriter and a mimeograph machine,
later became the *Poston Chronicle,* which served the Center until disbursement.

—Poston Collection, courtesy University of Arizona Library.

analysts in "studying" the deteriorating morale of the largest camp in America.

"For one thing, coming, as many of the administrators did, with the desire to build something better for the evacuees, it was very hard to find themselves powerless to relieve much of the suffering which they saw, and it was still harder to bear the brunt of the antagonism engendered in the residents. The lack of supplies and the fizzling out of plans bothered some of the administrative officers more than it did anybody else. Reaction of irritation appeared among those who were people-minded. It was felt that the residents were not being realistic about the situation they were in, while bickering among themselves and making demands on the Administration for the moon, were not taking advantage of the opportunities they did have. . . ."[1]

The "people-minded" management personnel and the more farseeing of the trained sociologists and anthropologists were overruled and brushed aside. The Director and Assistant Director had decided that a "get tough" policy was what the camp most needed.

Division of authority between the Indian Bureau and the WRA was a constant irritation, and a demoralizing factor in intelligent management of the camp. "Poston received orders, information, notices and inquiries from both offices that were uncoordinated and confusing. Similarly, it was often a puzzle to know where to send outgoing business. Thus, to the other frustrations and uncertainties of the situation in Poston was added the burden of divided loyalties which is always a very serious and incapacitating matter for the very people who are otherwise most able to give efficient service and faithful service."[2]

Along with all this frustration came a sudden change in Relocation Authority policy. During the summer the directorship of WRA had passed from Milton Eisenhower to Dillon S. Myer, a very able and promising administrator from Falls Church, Virginia, with many years' experience in the Department of

[1]See Leighton, *The Governing of Men*, p. 150.
[2]*Ibid.*, p. 151.

Agriculture—serving, up to the time of his appointment as Acting Administrator of the Agriculture Conservation Adjustment Administration. By fall it had become known that Mr. Myer wanted to see the newly built Relocation Centers dissolved, and all the evacuees permanently resettled in other parts of the United States "where there were no restrictions."

Added to Poston's top-level confusion was the hand the Federal Bureau of Investigation began taking in ferreting out the malcontents and the loudmouths. The problem of the FBI informers in Poston became a sudden and explosive one. These informers—the listening ears of the FBI—were known among the internees as *inus,* or dogs. To be suspected as a management stool-pigeon was a terrible and dangerous thing. To the Japanese mind, there was nothing lower than an *inu.*

The physical travail and mental suffering, always increasing rather than diminishing, kept Poston's makeshift hospital constantly full. The "Poston zephyrs," in which the savage, swirling desert winds laid their gritty filth into every shelf and corner of the tarpapered tenements were bad enough. But the coughings and the wheezings were indicative of the fact that emphysema, tuberculosis, and that dreaded form of desert silicosis, already endemic in the Army camps, were alarmingly present, and aggravated by the wind-blown dust.

Many of the Issei oldsters refused the Anglo-style of medical treatment, and fought constantly against availing themselves of even the modest facilities offered by Poston's dedicated and tireless Japanese doctors and nurses. From a medical standpoint the camp had been understaffed from the beginning. The *nihonjin* physicians who had come into Poston with the evacuation dragnet, and the coterie of trained nurses, had never, even at pittance pay, failed to render endless and dedicated service to their people.

But there were the Isseis who preferred the more ancient forms of healing, as practiced in the Japan they so fondly remembered. *Hari* and *moxa* practitioners had emerged, and these were secretly courted by many old people in preference to the Poston hospital. The *hari* practitioner, with the aid of various

[108

needles, ranging in size from one to six inches in length, with points graduated down to the size of a human hair, pricked the flesh at various points of the anatomy. Among the Isseis great efficacy was claimed for this treatment, through needle stimulation of the nerves leading to the affected parts. Now, also, many of the oldsters were wearing new *mogusa* or *moxa* scars. Like the *hari* treatment, it had for its premise the stimulation of the nerves, and with this stimulation, healing. The burning of punk or *mogusa*, on certain parts of the body was a favored form of medication among the Isseis, and said to be efficacious in the healing of every disease known to man.

It was also a favored form of discipline for fractious children. Many an American-born Nise could show his or her *moxa* scars as punishment. The wilder Nisei colts could show plenty of them.

Anma, in Japan, was another popular form of treatment. The practice was based on stimulation of the circulatory system by skillful massage. To the more modern Niseis it probably made better sense than these other forms of folk medicine. The only problem was that its practitioners were few, even in Japan, because custom decreed that they should be blind men—the theory being that blind people invariably developed an acutely perceptive sense of touch. In *anma* the touch was everything. But the only blind men in Poston seemed to be the *hakujins* at Management and the Fiscal Office.

Poston wallowed through its problems into November. And through these wretched and worrisome weeks, the great contest in North Africa was decided by half a million Allied soldiers. On the other side of the world, Admiral Halsey's fleet was thwarting Japan's all-out attempt to recapture the Solomons. Poston, it seemed, was forgotten in this bitter war. And gloom, uncertainty, and open rebellion, hung over the camp like an ugly pall.

Poston's directors were now consistently and frequently declaring to its citizens' committees that they were pushing Washington for the release of funds to more regularly and consistently pay the internees. Fiscal Office, with worried ear attuned to the portents, was convinced this was so. All one could do was pray that the money might be forthcoming before the camp exploded.

With Poston so continuously on edge from inner stress, there were bound to be news leaks and doom stories. Everyone, from camp inmates to management, were constantly distressed by the cruel and distorted way the California and Arizona press were handling the internal writhings of their community. Work slowdowns and protests were instantly interpreted as uprisings and sabotage. In Arizona, milk was in short supply because of the vast military demands. The internees at Poston and Gila camps were being caricatured by certain newspapers as "little brown enemies," pampered and fed by the government. While Arizona babies cried for milk they could not have, the indolent and healthy "Japs" were reported to never be in want for this or any other commodity.

Never was it mentioned that Poston internees were subsisting on a per capita food budget of thirty-seven and one-half cents a day.

The efforts which Miles E. Cary, Poston's director of education, was making to get some of the older Japanese American students back into the college education from which they so abruptly had been thwarted, was misinterpreted and attacked.

"Resentment was also expressed in the press at the luxurious education which the residents were supposed to be receiving. The fact that private funds supported some seminar courses sponsored by St. John's College was twisted to appear as if the Federal Government were spending money on silly experiments in education. The University of Arizona refused to cooperate in any plan to continue the college education of the evacuees, and its President gave as the reason, 'These people stabbed us in the back at Pearl Harbor.' "[3]

For the benefit of the internees who, for twelve dollars per month or less, went every day to man Poston's railroad ware-

[3]See Leighton, *The Governing of Men*, p. 144.

house at Parker, and the truckers who hauled in its daily supply, a barber shop had posted a sign, "Jap, Keep Out, You Rat!" Sensing the inchoate dissatisfaction throughout the camp, and worried at the signs of incipient rebellion, the Project Directors were leaning heavily on the FBI. Already they had alerted the Army command to the possible necessity of additional help. Mr. Collier's academically trained analysts were expertly sniffing the portents like single-track beagles. The internees considered the whole pack of them as spies. Security guard was doubled.

The camp was resentful of management's use of informers, and was paralyzed before the specter of them. Internees were certain that these "pigeons," mostly favor-seduced Kibeis and Niseis, had been strategically sowed throughout the camp. No one knew whom to trust. The job of the *inus* was to gather evidence against the"agitators"—whom management was convinced were causing the work slowdown, and were feeding the growing rebellion.

Because the community analysts consorted with the upper echelons of management, their training and good intentions were nullified through the natural suspicion of the internees as to whose side of the struggle they were representative. Inwardly the people were crying for someone other than managment or experts. They most desperately needed souls they could trust, who could talk in their behalf. Instead, no one in camp seemed capable of bridging the inscrutable wall of the races.

Meanwhile, hurt and anger swelled into ugly incidents. The free and easy camaraderie, that had eased them over their earlier misfortunes, was vanished. Everywhere now, men were suspectting their neighbors of being the informers, the spies, *the inus,* the dogs, who worked for the *hakujin* bosses against their own people.

Poston had been a test for actual physical survival from the first day the Japanese had been dumped into its bedlam of misery. Through the summer months the heat had been insufferable, with dust, flies and mosquitoes given free entry through the paper walls, even after the windows were installed. Wallboard, weather-stripping, and mosquito netting had been promised by management. Air-conditioning, of course, was out of the question. Those things went only to resident personnel. The internees dug themselves cellars.

The mosquito netting arrived long after the summer had vanished. If the wallboard and weather-stripping ever reached Poston's warehouses, the internees never saw it. And, as fall advanced, the climate of the Colorado River Desert swung abruptly from one of the hottest spots on earth, to a chilling cold that penetrated to the marrow of one's bones.

But along with the discomforts, there was spectacular beauty to nature's sudden switch in moods. With fall the green and purples, stretching out like an oriental carpet through the immensity of their valley, changed to tans and browns and grays as frost raped the foliage at the same time it stung into the flesh of man. At night now the sky had become a celestial sweep of beauty. The stars, untold millions of them, hung low, and unbelievably bright, and the milky way was like a brush sweep of fluorescent paint, from horizon to horizon.

Along with nature's illumination, there were now the bonfires that were keeping Poston veritably aflame. Dozens and dozens of fires there were, tended constantly, where the cramped and chilled internees gathered for warmth and conversation, because the stoves that had been promised by management, like the now even more desperately needed wallboard and weather-stripping, had never arrived.

There was a beauty in the night sky; a visual wonder and warning in the fires. And there was a glory in the day, could one have been rid of the frustration, worry and fear that tugged at one's bowels. There was a wild sort of loveliness in this world's lost corner, apparent even when one crawled out of the morning's blankets cold, numb, and utterly discouraged. And the fires of Poston, fed on mesquite and creosote brush, and the mountains of building scrap, were fast becoming the council centers of frustration, and the sound circles of the Issei and Kibei agitators. But in them, like the Indians of earlier America, the

Japanese were discovering that fires could do more than warm the flesh. Here was talk, stimulus, excitement. At the fires was something for *nihonjins* in every level of thought.

To evacuees, back at Santa Anita, Poston had been pictured as the honor city, where its occupants would tarry only long enough for arrangements to be made for their assimilation into the great body of American citizenry out and beyond the vulnerable areas of the coast. Unlike Manzanar and Tule Lake, there was to be no barbed wire encirclement.

Attempts to move families eastward, to export the labor force of Poston, and the granting of travel permits, had been sporadic, farcical, and finally abandoned altogether. Then the new push had been to set up Poston with cooperatives—farming, poultry, and cattle raising. But no implements had arrived, no breeding stock, and nothing whatever to start the poultry projects. Lumber and wire were impossible to obtain for the internees. Fiscal Management had a dozen explanations. But lumber *had* arrived for the tarpapered shacks. And there was sufficient wire on hand to put twelve miles of encirclement around all three units of Poston.

A poem, written by some unnamed Nisei, freely circulated, read at the fire circles, and posted on the block bulletin boards, mirrors the anguish:

THAT DAMNED FENCE

They've sunk the posts deep into the ground
They've strung out wires all the way around.
With machine gun nests just over there,
And sentries and soldiers everywhere.

We're trapped like rats in a wired cage,
To fret and fume with impotent rage;
Yonder whispers the lure of the night,
But that DAMNED FENCE assails our sight.

We seek the softness of the midnight air,
But that DAMNED FENCE in the floodlight glare
Awakens unrest in our nocturnal quest,
And mockingly laughs with vicious jest.

With nowhere to go and nothing to do,
We feel terrible, lonesome, and blue:
That DAMNED FENCE is driving us crazy,
Destroying our youth and making us lazy.

Imprisoned in here for a long, long time,
We know we're punished—though we've committed
    no crime,
Our thoughts are gloomy and enthusiasm damp,
To be locked up in a concentration camp.

Loyalty we know, and patriotism we feel,
To sacrifice our utmost was our ideal,
To fight for our country, and die, perhaps;
But we're here because we happen to be Japs.

We all love life, and our country best,
Our misfortune to be here in the west,
To keep us penned behind that DAMNED FENCE,
Is someone's notion of NATIONAL DEFENCE![4]

Physical imprisonment was bad enough, but it was the internal surveillance that was tearing the heart out of this camp. Management had, without thought of consequences, turned to the FBI for answer to work slowdowns, and reluctance of the internees to silently accept their degrading role as prisoners. The insidious betrayals by the *inus* had been followed by a wave of beatings and reprisals. Those suspected of being informers were secretly watched by the internees themselves, and one after another they were being set upon in the night, snatched from their beds by masked gangs, ambushed at dark corners, and brutally beaten. Incident after incident had occurred, to baffle the intelligence officers, and to provide a real investigative challenge for the FBI.

The attacks, the rumors, the suspicions and distrust now sweeping the camp were hideous things for both inmates and management. Worse, most of the victims of this new and secret brutality were American-born Japanese. Instead of the hoped-for

[4]Poston Papers, Special Collections Dept., Library, University of Arizona.

[114

democratic self-government, the cleavage between the Isseis and Niseis was growing ever wider, and the night fires were peppered with the haranguing of bitter discontents, and the new and alarming emergence of a pro-Japan element; seemingly backed up by the long-silent and long-neglected oldsters.

One had only to choose his fireside, to find talk rattling on any one of the alarming cleavages that had beset this vast and unreal world. "One type of fire group was exclusively men, Isseis, with a sprinkling of Kibeis. Their talk easily ran from their current discomforts and blaming the Administration, to blaming the Niseis even more and pointing out that most of the evil, from evacuation down to the lack of stoves, was due to mishandling by Nisei leaders, especially the Japanese American Citizens League. They were weak, it was said, did not know how to stand up for their rights and needed the leadership of the older people. There was evident resentment at having their juniors in years, experience and social position occupy places both in self-government and jobs. . . ."[5]

The Isseis, and to a lesser extent the Japan-educated Kibeis, had at last found voice, and in some circles it was definitely pro-Japan. They spoke warmly and fervently of the motherland, and castigated the unfeeling Niseis because they knew so little and cared so little about it. Since America had betrayed Japanese Americans, and wanted no part of them—why cooperate? Why work; why try to please? It would be better, they argued, to just sit out Poston until war's end, and then all, parents and children, move back to Japan.

Despair and frustration had weakened Issei ties with America, and was driving them into fantasies regarding the warm and beautiful nation from whence they once so gladly had fled. Mystic sentiment, and ceremonious culture of ancient Nippon now seemed more important than raising gayule or weaving camouflage nets as virtual prisoners of war.

In other fire circles were the rowdies, disillusioned by the evacuation, the threat of barbed wire, the Work Corps, the *inus*,

[5]See Leighton, *The Governing of Men*, pp. 155-156.

115]

and the old people. They wanted action—not inaction. They wanted to strike. They yearned to beat hell out of the informers; tear down the fences. They were as fed up with the WRA as they were with the emperor and his Issei windbags. "A third type of cluster was composed of Niseis, young men and women together, or at different fires. To a large extent, they were sore at everything. They were annoyed and uneasy about the talk of their parents and other Isseis, and they were equally bitter about the treatment they had received from the American public, Government and the Poston Administration. . . ."[6]

Although the old people accused them of running the camp, and selling out for favor, the Niseis were probably the most bewildered and futile segment of the lot. Their power in Poston, in spite of the fact that they manned most of the jobs, had never been much. But now, even that was on the decline. Their elected officers had batted and bruised their heads against Anglo misunderstanding and distrust. All efforts at self-government foundered on the schisms of the people themselves, and the wide gulf between internees and management. Through their contacts with administration, they had not been able to deliver the trust and tranquility which the camp so desperately needed. They couldn't control the threats. They couldn't allay the suspicions. Self-government, insofar as they were concerned, had failed.

Now, to them, there seemed to be no protection. The *inu* assaults were directed either against Niseis, or the American-born, Japan-schooled Kibeis. Management had demanded that Niseis deliver up to them the perpetrators of the secret beatings. This they were powerless to do. Niseis lived in a climate of racial cleavage and dissension. It seemed hopeless to try to serve masters who, themselves, were frustrated and divided in thought, and paralyzed in action.

The little *Poston Chronicle* tried to talk reason and sense. But all attempts seemed nullified because of the inner-office tug-of-war concerning proper handling of the rapidly approaching

[6]*Ibid.,* p. 158.

crisis. No problems could be equitably solved because the dual management, by the Indian Office and WRA, was hopelessly inoperative. Indecision and conflicting directives negated operations when firmness was needed. Stupidity, and complete inability to read the portents of the gathering storm, prevented any real approach to mutual understanding. When sympathy and rapport were needed, harshness and discipline was the answer.

While Fiscal Office churned in conflict, the fires burned.

POSTON POLICE
Members of the police department carve themselves riot clubs.

—*WRA Photo, National Archives.*

CHAPTER SEVEN

BY NOVEMBER the more spectacular fires up and down Poston's blockways threatened to incinerate the whole community. The more thoughtful and sensitive internees were not too preoccupied with their own problems to ignore the sure signs of incipient rebellion.

The Isseis, long silent and impotent as a group, because of the strident English-speaking Niseis who managed the camp and filled nearly every community job, had suddenly become brave and brazen. It was mostly Isseis now who harangued the crowds at the campfires. And, because of Japanese parental deference, there had been little done to silence them.

The suddenly erupted crisis came after a surprise visit to Poston of the WRA supreme boss, Dillon Myer. He had stopped over, on his way to Salt Lake City for a special conference on Relocation problems. He couldn't have shown up at a more crucial time, nor have left Poston in a greater state of confusion.

There had been *inu* beatings, and there had been suicides, but two nights before the arrival of Dillon Myer had come the incident which finally blew the camp apart. In Block 14, of Poston I, there was a bunkhouse solely occupied by bachelors. From the camp's beginning this quarter had been a scene of noise and tumult. In this bunkhouse, on Saturday night, November 14, Kay Nishimura, a thirty-year-old Kibei, was all but beaten to death by a mob of hooded young assailants. They stormed the bachelor quarters shortly before midnight. With lengths of pipe, lethally and savagely laid on, they had attacked Nishimura. As with previous *inu* incidents, the assailants had disappeared into the night.[1]

One looks in vain for news of any revolutionary tone in the columns of the camp newspaper during these early weeks of November. News reporters on the now daily *Chronicle* had long ago discovered that writing for a "kept" newspaper was a lot different from the free and easy press coverage of prewar California, and especially from the Japanese point of observance one had found in the Los Angeles *Rafu Shimpo* and San Francisco's *Japanese Daily News,* or the *Ofu Nippo* of Sacramento.

Later, and in retrospect, the report of William Kir-Stimon, an eastern based Relocation Officer, would indicate the ethereal thinking of management in Poston's growing time of trouble: ". . . Dr. Powell suggested the broadcasting of OWI news records in Japanese to weekly audiences in Poston; a mild, but characteristically negativistic, response was forthcoming. The Isseis want news releases, but they would not like biased American news thrust upon them. Block affairs are Issei-dominated to a large extent; 'official' American news in either Japanese or English would not be welcomed in the blocks . . .

"Unfortunately, the two newspapers that are generally available and generally read in Poston, the Los Angeles *Times* and the *Examiner,* are both anti-evacuee and nationalistic . . . Couldn't the Community Enterprise staff see that papers that are more civilized, such as the Los Angeles *News* and the San Francisco *Chronicle,* are regularly on sale in the canteens? . . .

"Rumors are by no means the problem they once were. Furthermore, I can see no practical way to establish a rumor clinic or propaganda analysis group, as such. At present, the Reports Office handles the refutation of many unfounded rumors, through the *Poston Chronicle* . . ."[2]

[1] See "War Relocation Authority Quarterly Report," Oct. to Dec. 1942; FBI files, Box 2. Poston Collection, University of Arizona Library.

[2] See "Poston Community Analysis Report No. 5," Poston Collection, University of Arizona Library.

Inu beatings and factional turmoil were given scant space in Poston's tiny, mimeographed, and closely censored news sheet. Its reporters had, at the very least, nodding acquaintance with Kay Nishimura. They knew his reputation among the internees as an agitator and political climber. Having been educated in Japan, with background as an American, Nishimura had made himself valuable to the Reports Officer, but insofar as they knew, only in translating Japanese documents found in camp.

Most of the internees had no way of knowing whether or not Kay Nishimura was an *inu*. But apparently there were too many who thought he was. Management's reprisal to the bloody assault was hard and it was swift. Fifty suspects were rounded up and thrown into Poston's jail. The Judo Club was suspected of being the motivating center for the activists. It was common knowledge that this young man's group, besides teaching grappling proficiency on the mats, harbored plenty of hate for the *inus*.

But the jailings did not stop the beatings. Next night, it was the parents of Hatsusi Yamada. Yamada was a twenty-nine-year-old Kibei.[3] And others were being warned and threatened. Meetings of management, analysts, and Citizens' Council were hastily called in an attempt to deal with the situation. In midst of the worry and flurry, Dillon S. Myer and his Washington entourage arrived. Not far behind Mr. Myer, and probably unknown to him, were additional officers from the FBI, dispatched to Poston to keep watch over the explosive situation.

Coolest and wisest heads in the crisis proved to be the academic advisers and analysts, headed by Dr. Alexander H. Leighton and Dr. E. H. Spicer, both highly accredited anthropologists. From the first, because they worked with management, and under the direction of John Collier of the Indian Bureau, these men had been eyed with coolness and skepticism by the internees. Now the moment had arrived where some expert advice was needed.

[3]See "War Relocation Authority Quarterly Report," Oct. to Dec. 1942; FBI file, Box 2. See also "Chronology of Poston Incident," p. 2, Poston Collection.

Mr. Myer, as National Director of the WRA, and as could be expected, immediately closeted himself with the Caucasian personnel. It is possible that he was never even briefed on the problems already turning the camp into open revolt. At the staff meeting in the morning, privy to Wade Head, John Evans, Ralph Gelvin, Nell Findley, the project directors, and the analysts, his remarks were almost totally concerned with his new concept for dispersal, the breaking up of the camps, and the assimilation of loyal Japanese Americans into the nationwide body of citizenry. He indicated to the camp managers that Poston was not to be made attractive. Industry no longer was to be established. Cooperatives were not to be the policy after all. Community and family roots were to be discouraged from implantation into Arizona soil. The camps, he insisted had been a mistake from the start. And the hoped-for dispersal was expected to be made happily and willingly.

Aside from talk that the Army was opening itself to Nisei enlistments, there appears to be no specific mention made as to where California "Japs," swindled out of their birthright, were to find family havens among American nationals who loathed sight of a Nipponese face. At the evening meeting, which internee committees, block managers, and camp representatives were allowed to share with management personnel, the WRA director's speech followed the same pattern and along the same issues. But this time Mr. Myer found himself running head-on into the desolate, querulous, and rebellious thinking of his Japanese charges.[4]

Much of the confusion stemmed from the fact that John Collier, Commissioner of Indian Affairs, had made a speech at Poston only weeks before. Collier's preachment, in substance, was diametrically opposed to the plans being enumerated by Mr. Myer. Here again—in open view even to Poston's populace —was that frightening and ambiguous puzzle of dual control. Collier, as head of the Indian Bureau, the governmental

[4]See "Chronology of Poston Incident," pp. 2 and 3. Poston Collection, University of Arizona Library.

agency operating Poston under contract from the WRA, had, in his speech, dwelt on the necessity for community stability, and the great and exciting plans ahead for Poston. Irrigation and land development, vast in scope, was in store for Parker Valley. The Valley was to be permanent new homeland for the Japanese Americans. John Collier had visioned ahead for forty years. For generations the internees would be living here, in free society—with their sons, and sons' sons.

But now, before them, was Dillon Myer, supreme head of WRA, preaching dispersal, admitting failure of the relocation camps, and telling the sad and confused internees that they must soon seek new homes among the cities and communities farther east. None of the exciting plans for Poston, so long prated by management, were to become realities. No cooperatives, no industry—nothing but fenced-in dry rot—while opposing government bureaucrats decided which path lay ahead for twenty thousand ethnic prisoners.

Confusion's storm from Mr. Myer's speech was inevitable. Even *hakujins* in management personnel joined with the internees in demanding answers to some pointed questions as to what lay ahead for Poston community. Dispersal was now the objective, if the WRA director were to be believed in preference to the Collier soporifics. But in this hour, the camp was seething with turmoil, and grave questions were crying for instant answers. "When do we, as members of the Work Corps, get paid?" "What about more doctors, and decent hospitalization?" "Why is the fence going up around the camps?" In the notes that remain of the Poston meeting, there is no indication that Mr. Myer openly discussed or even commented on the *inu* beatings, the fifty men in jail, or the fires and their bitter speeches.

The fifty prisoners were questioned all that Saturday night. Sunday morning they returned to their blocks, free men, but sullen and angry. There had been insufficient evidence to hold the Judo Club cronies for the barbarous assault. But this time the Reports Officer and Security Police were determined to ferret out the guilty ones and track down the ferment and sedition.

123]

George Fujii, and Isamu Uchida, instructors at the Judo School, and popular among the young men, were rearrested, and charged with felonious assault.

There were those at management who were obsessed with the idea that a gigantic Pro-Axis conspiracy existed at Poston. And it is true, there *was* preaching around the fires of hopes and conviction that Japan would win the war. Other *hakujin* members of management blamed the dual control of WRA and the Indian Bureau, the orders and countermands, the vacillation, and the broken promises to the internees. This agitation had come about, they were convinced, solely because of the bitterness of the evacuation, deprivation of rights, the trampling of dignity, and the stupidity of the WRA.

As to the beating incident, the mass arrests, and the final charges against the two men, only the strong-muscled youths who frequented the Judo center could have named or even have had passing interest in George Fujii or Isamu Uchida. But by Sunday night these two men, securely locked in Poston jail, had become the folk heroes of a drama of liberation. And forty-eight other released suspects now walked in pride among their fellows for having had their fragmentary share of the catalytic glory of the moment.

No longer now was it a matter of right or wrong; of wisdom or stupidity. It was the time for striking back at the *hakujin* for all the hurts. It had come—faster than one·could have expected—a latent violence awaiting only the moment of release. The fires, now stoked with increasing fury, were the gathering points of strength. A bleeding and battered *inu*—the informer—the dog—was trigger to its action. The courageous Judo boys, unfairly jailed, were suddenly the heroes. The marching chant was for their immediate vindication and release.

On the morning of November 18, Jim Yohira and a committee of seven internees called on Project Director Wade Head, to lay before him the more immediate grievances that were tearing Poston apart. One of their most desperate requests was for the release of Fujii and Uchida, and the dropping of all charges against those internees being picked up by the security guards, at behest of the FBI. Mr. Head who, with his deputy director Ralph Gelvin, was due to leave for Salt Lake City with Mr. Myer, and tied up with last-minute conferences, directed the committee to John Evans, as acting director, and suggested that they take up their grievances directly with the FBI men in camp.[5]

At 10:30 a.m., Dillon Myer, Wade Head, Ralph Gelvin, and other top management officials, departed for Salt Lake City, leaving the camp to the direction of subordinates, the FBI, and community analysts. It would appear that Dillon Myer still was unaware of the storm that was brewing. Up to this late hour, he seems to have made no public acknowledgment of it.

Half hour after the dignitaries had departed, an ugly crowd gathered in front of the jail at Poston I. Speeches were made, urging a general strike in sympathy for the imprisoned Judo boys. Nishimura, victim of the last beating, was reported dying, and an equally wild rumor had it that Uchida was to be charged with murder, and that the two young and brave Japanese men were to be removed to Yuma by the FBI.

John Evans, now solely in charge of Poston, was besieged by complaining internees. He was showered with entreaties concerning the safety of other camp members already marked for beatings or worse. Evans was hemmed in with problems.

At the fires, and at most of the speeches, the Isseis were now in control. Up to this point, the Niseis had managed practically everything in camp. Before the day was out, every appointive and elective post in Poston I had seen resignation or abdication, with the exception of the Japanese police force and fire department. And their loyalties were becoming increasingly tenuous.

It was wildly reported that management and the FBI were calling in troops to cope with the threat of insurrection. If and when the Army arrived, the *nihonjin* policemen and firemen would most certainly go. There was genuine fear, especially among the Niseis, that the bonfires might, in blind anger, be

[5]*Ibid.*, p. 4.

DRYGOODS CANTEEN, POSTON I

Part of the general store at Poston I. The little Indian girl in foreground is reminder that the relocation center was built on lands of the Colorado River Tribes Indian Reservation.

—*Poston Collection, courtesy University of Arizona Library.*

spread to the bunkhouses or mess halls. The frenzy-howlers around the fires, and the massive and pugnacious mob surrounding the jail, seemed totally made up of the suddenly articulate Isseis.

"Oh, yes, there were young people in the crowds," says Nobu Shimahara. "But most of us were only listening and watching. And there was plenty going on."

The strike now was real and ugly. The only Japanese at work posts in the vast camp were the hospital attendants and nurses, and those manning the vital posts of supply and security. A sensible reporting of the strike story through the columns of the *Chronicle* would have shown far more wisdom than the shouting of *banzais* before hysterical and ill-informed Issei old men. But in this the Nisei staff found itself useless. The *Chronicle* was under the thumb of management. Instead of the story, it carried management's statements of threats and caution. What was happening was not the sort of grist that was proper for the camp news wheel. So the people got black and distorted verbal rumors instead of fact.

Mr. Evans, with his apparent conviction that Japs had been too freely coddled at Poston, was not caught unprepared. He was not unaware of the crowds massing around the jail and the Poston I police shack. It was late afternoon, and already Japanese music was blaring from loudspeakers the internees had suspended over the heads of the assemblage. The falsetto wails of the native singers and the off-key twang of native strings probably grated on his nerves as much as it was scruffing the feelings of the other *hakujins* in residence.

They were seeing a thousand Japanese — listening, talking, milling in fury—the cold November partially warmed by a dozen fires, the chill wind broken by blankets, canvas, tarpaper, set high on posts scrounged from the construction piles. Those who occupied the *shibai* theater stage, and those who harangued the crowd, were Issei oldsters.

Here was the first time Poston had ever seen its Isseis assembled as a group. Now they literally overwhelmed the younger

Niseis present, both in numbers and volubility. The old men were spewing Japanese with the staccato of a jackhammer, faster than many Nisei ears could follow, and accompanied by the almost suffocating falsetto and tremolo dissonance from the loudspeakers. The whole scene was weird, unbelievable—a page from the farmers' rebellion of ancient Nippon.

Behind the orators, on the stage, painted on what appeared to be a bed sheet, was an immense dog. And the dog, in the drawing, was eating the bribe money paid by management. In the audience stood the block captains with white guidons on staffs, the block number skillfully executed in red circle, which at a distance could easily be taken for the bulls-eye dot of the Japanese flag. Nowhere did one see the American colors. And someone had hanged a soldier in effigy from a building window alongside. That was reason enough for the Niseis to tone down and fade out.

The smoke from the fires stung the eyes and choked in the throat. What seemed astonishing to those Niseis who could stomach the meeting was that nearly every face they saw was unfamiliar. It was as though a fresh but older crop of internees had suddenly entered the compound. The people they walked among, the intent, rheumy-eyed demonstrators, were strangers.

The fires had been built in huge pits, and were methodically stoked with scraps from the building operations, and the dried mesquite and creosote brush that had been cleared from the acreage, and piled high. "They'd issued us no stoves," says Henry Mori. "So the fires were the only means we had of keeping warm." Smoke stabbed at eyes and nostrils. The unmoving male Isseis who hugged the outer margins, with their blue-veined hands to the blaze, argued from a dozen divergent viewpoints.

The more thoughtful internees knew that all John Evans had to do was pick up a telephone. In an hour there would be enough jeeps and machine guns in Poston to settle the evacuee problem once and forever. Apparently the acting director was a patient man; in spite of the Issei firebrands and their vocal effusion. Those who had backed off from direct involvement were hoping that Evans would not mistake a strike for a rebellion; that, in spite of all, he would *still* listen to the basic pleas of the people. The mass meetings grew noisier and more voluble as the day progressed. Community analysts, at Fiscal Office, tried desperately to build logic into the reasons for the noise, the music, the confusion, and the tone of resistance and anarchy that had come into the once orderly and smooth-running camp.

The only progressive and logical thing that seemed to have occurred this day was that the people had assembled an entirely new board to represent them—seventy-two members—called the Committee of the People—and with the Isseis liberally a part. They, in turn, had chosen a grievance committee of twelve. In one of the block recreation halls, these representatives were spending that hectic afternoon preparing once again the people's case for presentation to Evans and the management.

But while the Committee endeavored to tame the hotheads and to painfully hammer out a defense, the music still blared, the effigy still dangled from the window. Anger and confusion long ago had replaced decorum and restraint. Management, in standing aloof from the turmoil, posed more threat and danger to the participants than if they had attempted to lower themselves to the turmoil. But, so far, the Army had not yet arrived.

Most of the politely silent Niseis, unlike the oldsters, the militant judoists, and the voluble and frenzied strike leaders, were drawing no warmth from the cause. Their own hurts had turned more to confusion than to hate. The pro-Axis undertones of what they were hearing and seeing vexed and disturbed them. This thing no longer could be passed off as a joke, and certainly management, with its stereotyped thinking, would see nothing light and humorous about the threats and epithets now drenching the air. No internee was conscious or aware of any full-scale alien plot to take over. For that reason alone, this sudden and mutinous emergence seemed incredible.

True, many an Issei, with wealth and livelihood swept away, humiliated and ignored in camp by the *hakujin* management,

NOTIONS COUNTER, STORE, POSTON I
The general store at Poston I was a popular spot in the Arizona Center.

—Poston Collection, courtesy University of Arizona Library.

and the brash and disrespectful Niseis, now longed for the old country from whence they had fled. But there had been few of them who had wanted or expected Japan to win the war. Whatever alien plot there was, if any, could have been engineered by only a comparatively few militants. The emerging Isseis were victims rather than possessors of these fangs of rebellion.

In late afternoon, management made its first move. Speakers were sent out to the mass meeting. It couldn't be Dillon Myer, Wade Head, or Ralph Gelvin, who were on their way to Salt Lake City. It was the Stetson-and-boots camp director, John Evans. He was followed by Doctors Alexander Leighton and E. H. Spicer, of the little group of professional stress monitors that Washington had sent to observe Poston, and to counsel with its management. Alongside the jingoistic old men, these experts appeared very young. But they carried themselves with authority, and the people knew it.

Internees politely turned off the Jap music while Evans and the analysts spoke. A Kibei linguist came along to translate the remarks so every Issei might understand. But the cat-calls and confusion that followed *hakujin* statements, and their translation, even though they were delivered in a friendly manner, and by intelligent men, indicated a reiteration of demands for social reform, release of the prisoners, and immediate work stop on the fence.

It was apparent in every way that the community analysts, at least, were sympathetic toward the internees in their needs and their hurts. But the crowd was in no mood to reason with the speakers on the necessity of orderly dispersal, the placing of their grievances to management through the freshly elected council, and the wisdom for holding the Judo heroes in custody until their guilt or innocence could be established.

It was anything but a friendly reception they gave their bosses. This was mob hysteria, like what had happened in reverse at Terminal Island, and from which there could be no reasoning. The hostility, the hanging effigy, and the banners with the

131]

strange devices, could not fail to impress these emissaries with the magnitude of the rebellion.

It was inevitable too that, before this day was finished, Poston's "uprising" would go out as news to the world. The American citizenry, heretofore completely ignorant and uninterested as to what went on in the concentration camps, now were shuddering at the knowledge, and grinding their teeth in fury as newspapers across the nation played up the unspeakably traitorous actions of those "Japs" out in Arizona. General feeling was that the fences ought to be ten feet higher.

And it was also inevitable that the Army should alert itself and move in, as Poston's loudspeakers resumed their blaring out of Jap music—louder and more defiantly than ever. The crowds had not followed Evans' orders to disperse and return to work— and the Isseis again harangued the crowd.

It was unfortunate that Dillon Myer had taken Wade Head and Ralph Gelvin from the camp. It was unfortunate that the FBI was on hand to ferret the *inu* beatings. It was tragic that the internees could not heed the calm and dispassionate counsel of the skilled and understanding analysts. For, before the sun went down on that turbulent November day, the Army was at the gates of Poston, and the militant internees were making ready to defend themselves with fists, clubs, and table knives.

Lined up at the gates were jeeps, weapons carriers, soldiers, and machine guns. One military vehicle moved through the sentried gates and had started into the compound before it was frantically stopped by some of the calmer heads from management. Leighton, Spicer, and Security Police Chief Kioshi Shigekawa, made frantic effort to dissuade the lieutenant commanding the Army platoon from entering Poston I. They argued that a show of force at this time was not only premature, but certain to precipitate ugly incident or bloodshed. Meanwhile the internees grimly made ready for battle.

Somehow, almost miraculously, the calm heads prevailed. After considerable *hakujin* vocal persuasion, the troops and cars withdrew. And Poston was left to stew another night in its own bitter juice.

But the fires still burned, the music still blared, and the people watched defiantly while jeeps and weapons vehicles drove around Poston I in a show of strength. It was intimidation, of course, even though the soldiers remained outside the camp. It was warning, not lost on the gaping, chattering people. But it was not yet bullets. And it was not yet death.

In spite of the fires, the crowds, the god-awful music—as long as the Peoples' Committee talked, as long as management had a listening ear, as long as the Army remained outside the gates— there still was hope.

OUTDOOR THEATER, POSTON

Scene of native Kabuchi drama, many enjoyable theatrical presentations and pageants, and convenient stage for Poston orators.

CHAPTER EIGHT

THE WEEK wore itself out in alarms and crises, and the strike continued. The meetings at management were stormy and bitter, with the new council and grievance committee consistent in their declaration that the elected representatives of the people had, for months past, been treated with complete indifference by the Caucasian heads. They maintained that democratic government at Poston had been a total farce. The management staff, critically reduced by the regional conference in Salt Lake City, were divided in opinion. Some wanted peace with the internees, on any and all terms that were honorable. Others wanted the Army in, the FBI stridently on the trail of every militant, and a show of force that would convince the Japs once and for all that America would tolerate neither strikes nor revolts in its camps.

The telephone lines were kept busy between Poston, Salt Lake City, and Washington. Even with the dignitaries absent, there was plenty of direction from Mr. Myer, Mr. Collier, and Mr. Head. But America's newspapers had latched on to the story, and the "revolt" at Poston had become a matter of national concern.

Poston was not alone in its problems. Other camps were seething with strikes and turmoil, all with the same common and almost identical reasons—the stress of evacuation, hardship, shame, and neglect. They were whipped to fury by the Issei-Nisei-Kibei internal conflict, WRA vacillation, and the inflammatory leadership of power-and-favor motivated politicians among the internees themselves.

Manzanar, the camp Poston residents dreamed longingly for, was likewise boiling in trouble. Joe Kurihari, a veteran of World War I who, after serving America with laudable patriotism and devotion, now found himself a prisoner of the nation for which he had dedicated himself. His crime was simply that, in the present war, he wore the wrong kind of face. Like other internees, he resented the affront to himself and to his fellow Japanese Americans. Unlike most of them, however, he transferred his inner rebellion into militant action.

At Manzanar, Kurihari attempted reorganization of the JACL, charging that it had become a tool of the American military, the WRA, and a pool for the *inus* to spy and inform on their fellow prisoners. His speeches were inflammatory because they were couched in open pride for the Japanese race, bitter criticism of American treatment of this minority, and, in the end, open denunciation of the war itself. He soon had gathered about him a group of agitators that blew Manzanar into a storm.

So, almost simultaneously with Poston's strike and rebellion, came the same bitter news out of Manzanar. It was like a replay of the same record. A Nisei by the name of Fred Tayama was severely beaten as a suspected *inu*. Suspects were hauled into jail. Angry crowds assembled about camp — made angrier by Kurihari and his fellow agitators.

Manzanar Project Director, Ralph P. Merritt, attempted desperately to reason with the camp mobs. But, unlike Poston's initial hesitance and reticence, troops were immediately called in. The crowds were shoved away from Manzanar's police station and jail, and from that point the military confronted the howling and angry internees with rifles, bayonets and machine guns. When the people refused to quieten or disperse, the soldiers donned their gas masks and made ready to move against them. At first the crowds retreated, but, harangued by activitists, they soon returned.

One of them, a Nisei with a brother serving in the United States Army, reputedly started the engine of a car nearby, headed the vehicle toward a machine gun, and jumped out. The troops opened fire—killing him. Another nineteen-year-old Nisei died three days later from gunshot wounds. Ten other internees were wounded in that deadly blast.

In Manzanar's tragedy, as in Poston's uprising, only a very small percentage of camp population were actively involved. At least ninety percent shared the turmoil only as interested spectators.

Nearly every one of the ten great relocation centers suffered from stress and turmoil, some with actual physical eruption, others with minor strikes and grumbling. Topaz Camp, in Utah, witnessed the gunning down of an elderly Issei by one of its sentries. And Tule Lake, with its over-share of incorrigibles, was later to know death and rebellion of tragic proportion. "Most of it could have been avoided," says Mr. K. "They didn't talk to us—and we couldn't talk to them."

But at Poston, the management strategy seemed geared to a deliberate avoidance of any further confrontations with the jingoistic Isseis constantly demonstrating in front of the jail. All talks and deliberations with the internees were confined to the management offices, with the Peoples' Committee doing the walking and the talking. Policy forbade the sympathetic *hakujin* personnel, or even the Washington sociologists, from courting friendship with the Japanese, so long as the strike lasted, or the camp was in rebellion.

On the concession side, work was stopped on the big fence, and Fujii was released from Poston jail to Poston custody. But the bosses were adamant about wanting to turn Uchida over to Yuma County for prosecution on attempted murder. No internee could remotely imagine a Jap getting fair trial in Arizona. On this, and other issues, the Committee angrily resigned, and then reconvened. The bosses gave little quarter, and the strike continued.

On Friday, November 20, a fleet of big trucks, bearing equipment and *hakujin* personnel to set up the new camouflage-net factory at Poston, pulled into camp. They found the camp so laced with rebellion that no men would work even at maintenance jobs, let alone at the ephemeral industries so constantly proposed and never materialized.

On Saturday, Captain McFadden, of General DeWitt's staff, arrived to observe Poston, should the Army find it necessary to forcibly bring its own brand of order. He found the Caucasian personnel in bitter disputation among themselves as to the best course in dealing with the impasse. Some wanted a ban on all Japanese language in the camp; some wanted every loudmouth and orator immediately rounded up and jailed. Some wanted a sympathetic listening to the grievances as presented by the Citizens' Committee. The only sensible act for the whole day was that Captain McFadden spent Saturday observing, rather than immediately calling in the troops. At the very least it saved Poston from a shooting tragedy such as those which were to forever scar Manzanar and Tule Lake.

No one realized, at the time, that this very lack of action would prove out as the wisest possible course. It had been a miserable, cold, and hectic week for everyone concerned — nihonjin and hakujin. With Wade Head absent, and no one sure, little had been accomplished one way or another. Hour after hour the fires had burned, the loudspeakers had ground out Japanese music, and the hotheads had harangued their dwindling audiences. But subtly, in spite of the music and oratory, a change had come over the camp. By Friday the red circled block pennants had vanished in favor of less suggestive figures drawn with black paint or ink. Effigies no longer dangled from windows. The Isseis were running out of steam. Niseis once more were swaggering confidently through camp.

Management, by a simple walking of the compound, could have observed the change, and taken heart. The old men, exhausted and wearied by their days of excitement, were returning to their go boards. The united front was degenerating into petty squabbles between Niseis, Isseis and Kibeis. Word was being passed that the Committee was winning out, and gaining concessions. Apathy and confusion of management was being in-

[138

terpreted as wisdom and restraint. All that was wanted—by everybody—was an honorable way out.

By letting it run its course, without openly fighting it, the strike, like a spinning top, was running down. Eventually it would topple, from spent inertia, and from its own weight. Saturday's mass meeting at the jail was as different from Monday's affair as day was to night. There was still the dissonant blare of music, but Poston's Isseis no longer controlled the speaker's stand. Now Niseis, without directly challenging the revered old men, were shouting their own new day. Uchida was to be tried in camp, instead of by hostile Yuma County. A new representative government was promised. More important, Washington, belatedly recognizing Nisei citizenship, was to actually start recruiting soldiers from Poston.

Now there were arguments and fist fights around the fires. Niseis were hunting down the pro-Axis agitators with the same zeal they had used in rooting out the *inus*. There was a change. One sensed it in the air.

At 1:30 a.m., Wade Head and Ralph Gelvin arrived from Salt Lake City. Even in the middle of the night, word passed that the Director again was at the helm. Lights burned for many hours at management after their arrival. Meetings and consultations were held. And, though neither of these supervisors had ever been noted for pro-Japanese sentiments, there was a sense of security and hope. Future meetings would be fair, the procedures would be honorable. Points of grievance no longer would be swept under the rug. Never again would the internees, through their representatives, be treated with contempt, or their travail ignored. Nothing but good would come out of this thing.

Sunday morning the internees crawled out of their blankets to the ever present chill of winter. But something about this morning was strangely different. It took a moment to be fully conscious of it. The shrill, falsetto music of Japan no longer was blaring from the loudspeakers. All was quiet.

And then suddenly music *did* come — but the song had changed. It had an American beat. Many an internee smiled, then laughed aloud, as he or she heard the song. It was "Praise the Lord, and Pass the Ammunition!" By that sound every internee knew that the "rebellion" was over.

* * * * *

After the strike, Poston was never quite the same. The Isseis, having found that their own voice and actions had saved them from complete oblivion, henceforth reacted in patterns dictated by their own outlook and experience. Some, principally those who had a working knowledge of English, accepted posts in the revitalized and more democratic self government of the community. In this new concept, all internees were winners in some way or another. Only those die-hard oldsters, those who were pro-Japan, or those who looked back with nostalgia to the peace and serenity of the Fatherland, crawled into cowed and silent groups, to await the day when they could be free of Poston forever.

The hard-core and more strident Isseis, those who had given up every hope of American equity and justice, their voices silenced by the upsurge of Nisei strength and American viewpoint, now retreated into mute and angry bitterness. Since, in their families, the male parent ruled the household, their paternal persuasions were often completely pro-Japan and pro-emperor. This was the Issei and Kibei type the FBI kept under constant surveillance. This was the internee who had most reason to fear the *inu*.

Even among the Nisei, the strike, with its measure of victory and conciliation, could not return all to serenity and justice. Their greatest hurt and humiliation was the fact that the government had never, in the year past, given them the least chance to prove their loyalty and patriotism. A war was being fought, they were citizens, but because they wore Nipponese faces, they had been sidelined and were suspect. With no sense whatever of national participation, they could not fail to sense their own brand of bitter fury. This, more than anything, had driven many of them into Poston's rebellious turmoil.

[140

Settlement of the strike, and the gradual return to normalcy, put men back to work. Again they plowed, planted, made bricks, dug canals, and sped the camouflage-net factory off to some kind of start. But the one morale-builder that hit Poston like a breath of spring, came when the government actually backed up its promise by opening an Army recruiting station at Poston I. That it would be successful was a foregone conclusion. The *Chronicle* proudly carried a listing of Poston's first inductees. When Niseis at last realized their citizenry was being recognized, they began walking again like men. Gone was haggling on the jobs, work stoppages, and the sad and sullen faces. Their country at last had found them, and was measuring them for their worth.

"At Poston, a lot of young guys like myself didn't make quick rush for Army enlistment," Nobu Shimahara remembers. "A lot of Niseis in camp were still sore about the evacuation, and the slowness of their government in recognizing our rights."

But, in general, the new feeling was here, and it was good. And there was more than a trace of pathos in this. Before Pearl Harbor there had never been a question as to any Nisei's right or duty to wear the American uniform. Prior to Japan's attack, they had been drawn into the services, by draft and enlistment, the same as every other citizen out of the American melting pot.

Before the bombs fell on Hawaii, college trained Japanese Americans had enjoyed and accepted the same opportunity to enroll for officer training as was granted any other talented or accomplished American. Scores of them had gone through Officers' Training School, and had earned their commissions. But with the shattering impact of sudden war, the American military had found itself with hundreds and hundreds of Japanese, already functioning in the service as officers and enlisted men.

Immediately after Pearl Harbor came the new policy—turn Japanese recruits away—refuse their entry into the armed forces, even under draft status. And, with the opening of hostilities, what to do with those already bearing arms became the government's nagging dilemma.

141]

Those homesick kids in uniform, whether they wore bar or stripe, who occasionally visited the ten internment camps, were those who had been caught up in service prior to the big roust, and the sons and husbands of the evacuees. They were angered at sight of their parents and wives uprooted and imprisoned. They were disturbed about their own uncertain status. As far as security would allow, they clarified to their worried kin some of the problems of the AJA servicemen (Americans of Japanese Ancestry) in the U. S. Army and Navy. What they told was at least partial answer as to why Niseis had for so long been denied enlistment privilege.

In a peculiar sort of way, these *nihonjins* in uniform were a privileged class, because the nation had wanted no more Japanese inductees. But out in Hawaii—there in the midst of bombs and treachery—the Army had been caught with two companies of National Guard—the 298th and 299th Infantry—fifteen hundred soldiers—nearly all of them wearing Jap faces. In spite of the fact that these Niseis were achingly patriotic and eager, the Army had felt impelled to sweep them under the rug.

No one knew for certain how AJAs would behave if Japan attempted a shore invasion. Stripped of their weapons, treated like prisoners of war, these two crack infantry companies had been herded aboard ship, and hauled to Oakland, California. There they had been put aboard trains and dumped at old Camp McCoy, in Wisconsin.

To avoid the horrendous risk of these AJAs capitulating to the armies of their cousins from Japan, they were kept safe and secure in Wisconsin, and then later hauled to Camp Shelby, in Mississippi. That was only one problem. The American army was already brownly seasoned with hundreds of other AJAs drawn pre-war from the farms, businesses, and professional circles of the once sizable population pocket of the Pacific Coast. In the Army, Navy and Marines, too were those AJA officers, chaplains, and doctors. But the decision had been made. Until Japs proved themselves as citizens, there would be no more. Up to now, locked in concentration camps, or assigned to the lowest menial capacity in the service, there had been little chance to make that proof.

Because the Hawaiian companies, based at Camp McCoy, and later at Camp Shelby, had behaved themselves, and had shown no signs whatever of traitorous thought or act, Washington minds had eventually decided that it might be wisdom to make use of this pool of manpower, by cranking it out as an all AJA corps, perhaps even staffed with Japanese field officers — the whole unit composed of those little brown bastards no American dared trust. Other AJA soldiers, suspect and lonely, had been drained out of the regular military and siphoned into Shelby.

The Hawaiian boys, in quaint perspective, called themselves *buddhaheads*—but they were good soldiers—gay, carefree, and tough. They, in turn, labeled the Japanese service men from the mainland as *kotonks*. The *kotonks*—embittered by the roust of their parents—were not nearly so gay and carefree. But all of these soldiers—to a man—resented being called "Japs."

The Battle of Midway was on in fury, and with the outcome in doubt, they had shipped those fifteen hundred AJAs from Hawaii to the mainland. The 298th and 299th Infantry had been replaced by regulars wearing the right kind of faces. On the docks at Oakland, this shipload of bewildered young soldiers had been called the "Hawaiian Infantry Battalion." They had been landed, stripped of weapons and armaments. As virtual prisoners, under military guard, they had been hauled out to Wisconsin.

The ruling already had been handed down that no soldier of Japanese ancestry was to touch or handle firearms. Thousands of enlisted and drafted AJAs were turned overnight into yard birds, clerical help, and commissary clerks. And every loyal Nisei who wore the uniform of his country resented this ignominy and this dishonor.

But the buddhaheads out of Hawaii had brought with them a pair of commanding officers—Anglo officers at that—Colonels Farrant Turner and Jim Lovell—who had known their men as National Guardsmen. At McCoy these officers held under their command fifteen hundred trained and seasoned soldiers, anxious to prove their loyalty, and bitterly resentful about their prisoner-of-war treatment.

Because Turner and Lovell had refused to allow their two superb companies of infantry to be turned into clerks and yard birds, the miracle had happened. At Camp McCoy, they had stood up for their men against every narrow-minded bigot. The COs turned out to be as tough and hard as their little Island yabos.

At McCoy, under these officers, the 100th Infantry Battalion Separate was born—out of the old 298th and 299th—and forged into a unit as dedicated to the art of war as their Samurain ancestors. At first they resented having kotonks assigned to their outfit. Buddhaheads, fiercely loyal to Hawaii and its background, wanted no mainland-born Japanese in their ranks. Out of this unresolved incompatability between islanders and mainlanders, came the decision to fashion later AJA units with geography in mind—either stateside or Hawaiian.

Through its *Chronicle*, Poston learned how well the Japanese soldiery had gotten along with the citizens of Wisconsin. Unlike California, in Wisconsin the AJAs had not been penalized for wearing the face of the enemy. When the local citizenry had realized that these little brown men were just homesick kids, rather than Nipponese terrorists, they had been accepted, and they had been liked.

The residents of Sparta and other towns around and adjacent to the base had been serenaded with ukelele bands, and soon were dancing to the island music of steel guitars. *Luauas* and shows, put together at the least hint of interest, had enlivened community after community throughout central Wisconsin. The regimental band, the string ensembles, the spectacular dancers of this strange outfit had been invited to the University of Wisconsin, at Madison. To the blare of island music from their band, crack units of the 100th had precision marched in the great football stadium, to the delight of the crowds at halftime.

Wisconsin had learned to love these "monkeyfaces." There had been genuine sorrow when they left.

It had been sadly different when the 100th was moved to permanent training quarters at Camp Shelby. Most of the men hated Mississippi. A dark skin—any dark skin—was anathema to its white populace. And a Japanese face—even a smiling Japanese face—had failed to prove entry into kindliness and fraternity. The AJAs had been even more resentful than Negroes about being heaved bodily out of Mississippi's bars, restaurants and toilets. But these tough little roosters had seldom been apathetic about it.

At Shelby the 100th had not only perfected its battle tactics, but had set the pace and tradition for other AJA units being formed from the sudden new rash of enlistments out of America's relocation camps. It was there they also had participated in one of the war's most peculiar battle experiments. As part of the D-Series Maneuvers, a detachment of the 100th was sent to Cat Island, near Gulfport. The government, or some Army brass-head, had spawned the idea that Japanese people carried their own peculiar body stench—maladorously different from that of one hundred percent Americans. Why not, the high command had concluded, gather up every husky and savage wolf-hound in America? Why not train these beasts in the art of ripping to pieces every Jap they met Why not leave it to the perceptive canine sense to differentiate between Japs and Anglos?[1]

So, hundreds upon hundreds of dogs, from all across America, had been enlisted in another tremendous war effort. Everyone who owned a German Shepherd or similar, and wanted to be especially patriotic, had relinquished the family hound toward the greater glory of chewing up the enemy. On the premise that Japs somehow smelled different than pure Americans, the program was built. The AJAs detailed to Cat Island were to prove this essential point.

[1]For details on the Cat Island experiments, see Thomas D. Murphy, *Ambassadors In Arms*, pp. 92-93. University of Hawaii Press.

Cat Island, Mississippi, had been especially selected as promising spot for those exercises in canine warfare. In its swamps, and snake-infested boglands, near Gulfport and Hattiesburg, was the ideal replica of the Asiatic frontiers in which Americans already were fighting and dying. On Cat Island, it was decided, packs of killer-trained dogs would be loosed to seek out Japs in the jungleland. It was expected the beasts would instinctively know the difference between friend and foe—strictly by smell. The Army had Cat Island—it had the sweet smelling Americans—it had the dogs. From its 100th Infantry, it had plenty of the more foully-odorous Japs.

Not until the AJAs were issued padded suits and face guards, and their rifles traded for riot clubs as the sole means of defense, had they realized what was expected of them in this part of D-Series. They were deployed into the swampy jungle. The dogs were loosed. If this phase of D-Series war games proved successful, it might well mean a turning point in the Asian struggle.

Neither buddhaheads nor kotonks would ever likely forget Cat Island. With the baying of the hounds, it had been like a replay of *Baskerville,* or an oriental version of *Uncle Tom's Cabin.* The dogs had come up, snarling and vicious. The fear-stink must have been Jap all right. At the first assault, they had been forced to form rings, clubs in hand, for the defense of their very lives. There were casualties to dog-bite, as they had struggled to defend themselves against the lunging and snarling beasts.

After they had hauled the quota of AJAs to the hospital for stitches and Pasteur shots, the dog maneuvers had been abandoned as another brasshead dream. The dogs, it seemed, never *could* learn to properly differentiate between *nihonjin* and *haku-jin.* After tasting human blood, and scenting men in the jungle, any man—any flesh—any blood—had been all the same to the dogs. They had been as quick to devour their American G.I.s as they were their Nipponese counterparts. Final decision was to use the dogs for guard duty and prisoner detention.

While the AJAs were being hammered into respectable and dependable soldiery at Shelby, in Mississippi, the AJAs in America's ten concentration camps were just as quietly knuckling down to the changing and oftentimes confusing pattern of conduct laid out for them by their bosses. Settling of the tumultous strike had cooled off Poston's internal problems, even though it had failed to remove the basic hurts spawned and intensified by the evacuation. The WRA, under Dillon Myer's direction, at last cognizant of the vast ideological cleavage tearing at flesh and thoughts of the people, began making it possible for them to more clearly define their standings as fellow humans, and to act a little more in the direction of their motivation.

One serious aftermath of the Poston uprising had been the determined interrogation by government sociologists of the Japanese holdouts. Many Isseis were now requesting transfer to Tule Lake—California's high security camp for aliens and incorrigibles. With Poston now swinging so patriotically to the other arc of the pendulum, the recalcitrant oldsters and bitter losers had become isolated and alone.

Opening of Army and Navy enlistments for Niseis had made a profound change in Poston's climate. Once again citizenship was being recognized and accepted. From Camp Shelby came announcement that another all-Japanese army was being built—patterned after the renowned 100th. The response among the young men was most encouraging.

The *Chronicle* was cognizant of this profound change in the camp, and made note of it. In December came an issue commemorative of the tragedy of Pearl Harbor, and mentioned with interest and pride, not only the basic reaction of Niseis when tendered an opportunity to serve their country, but in the astonishing success of war bond drives and blood bank campaigns.

On February 8 of the new and happier year of 1943, the WRA began its "loyalty" registration, for the combined purpose of serving the Army recruitment program, and for clearance of leaves in the first move of the bureau's hopes to phase out the camps as anachronisms born of baseless fears and hysteria. It

147]

was Question 28 of the "loyalty" interrogation which now shook the internees. To AJAs everywhere, this query became the final separation between America and the Fatherland.

"Will you swear unqualified allegiance to the United States of America," the question demanded, "and faithfully defend the United States from any or all attack by foreign forces, and forswear any form of allegiance and obedience to the Japanese emperor, or any other foreign government, power, or organization?"[2]

By this act, the WRA, without realizing it, and however well-intentioned, had laid another time bomb under every relocation camp in America.

During the crucial months American troops were securing Guadalcanal in the bitter and attritious struggle with Japan, Question 28 of the loyalty test was plowing its deep furrow through the camps. But no matter which facet the worry, the inductee list published in the *Poston Chronicle* was fat.

"We went in because we were glad for the opportunity to go in," declares Mr. K. "It was like saying 'here is one young man willing and unafraid to swallow bitterness. Here is a Jap-faced American. But this Jap-faced American is a good American.' They shipped us off to Phoenix and Los Angeles by charter bus. Eventually most of us landed in Mississippi, at Camp Shelby."

Week after week the bus hauled its load of inductees out of Poston, packed with happy, noisy boys, yearningly anxious to prove that Niseis were Americans in spite of their faces. The same scene was being duplicated in every other relocation camp. The internees knew that re-acceptance of Japanese into military service had been the best thing that ever happened. Proudly, and at very opportunity, the *Chronicle* continued its story of "our boys."

[2]See WRA Community Analysis Section, Notes No. 1, p. 1. Poston Collection, University of Arizona Library.

CHAPTER NINE

THE ULTIMATE fate of Poston and the nine other ugly and sprawling relocation camps hung precariously through the earlier months of 1943. Acting on the conviction as expressed on his brief visit to Poston in November, and in the Salt Lake directorial conference, Chief Dillon Myer petitioned Secretary of War Stimson, in March, for relaxation of the harsh exclusion orders against the Japanese. By now the knowledge that the WRA Director planned the elimination of the barbed wired monstrosities had percolated through management thinking at each of the great centers. The farms, the cooperatives, the industries such as camouflage netting and parachute manufacturing, were either half-heartedly pursued, or held in abeyance, while top decision was being made. But Myer's dream of emptying the camps, and the more useful absorption of Japanese Americans into the nation's citizenry, was summarily rejected by the Secretary of War.

In April, a congressional subcommittee investigating the WRA, headed by Senator A. B. Chandler of Kentucky, made the recommendation to Dillon Myer for *tighter* surveillance of the internees. Instead of emptying the camps, it was suggested that their "disloyal" members be segregated and transferred to maximum security. Secretary of War Henry L. Stimson answered Dillon Myer's petition for phasing-out of the camps, with an adamant reaffirmation of the Military Exclusion Order. "A serious deterioration of evacuee morale has been noted in recent months," Stimson replied. "This unsatisfactory development appears to be the result in large measure of the activities of a vicious, well-organized, pro-Japanese minority group to be found at each relocation project."[1]

It did not matter that the strikes and the tumult had subsided. Unlike Mr. Myer, Mr. Stimson was not cognizant of the fact that camp affairs were now comparatively placid, and most encouragingly hopeful. Mr. Stimson emphatically noted that "Pro-Japanese" militants had stirred up trouble. They had worried the Western Defense Command. The refusal was pointed and direct. This was not the time for dispersal.

So, before summer arrived, Director Myer, in compliance, had reluctantly instituted the program of transferral to Tule Lake of all Japanese nationals, and those whose thinking on the war effort might be suspect. Poston, like the other camps, suffered through the ensuing witch hunt. But the quest had been made easier of accomplishment by the stark revealment of November's "uprising," and by the "loyalty" registration, with its bald and incriminating Question 28.

The decision of many oldsters to voluntarily transfer their families to Tule Lake was sharp and poignant indication of the under-stress. A war of flame and death was one thing, but the casualties of this hideous conflict were not all in battle. It seemed incredible the change that had come over some of the internees.

Children, one by one, in true Japanese fashion, followed the adamant counsel of their parents. And, by so doing, they gave forfeit to the one thing they had once held most dear—their citizenship in America. To hesitate, was to defy one's father. Cradled in the tradition of Issei parenthood, but torn by the Nisei urge to freedom, it was no easy thing nor happy time for many a young AJA.

Worried and helpless, friends and relatives crowded the hearing room at Poston Administration, while their men faced the final interrogation. Many a Nisei or Kibei stood white-faced and

[1]See Dillon S. Myer, *Uprooted Americans,* p. 165.

defiant before the three-man board. To them, the hearing was the end of the line; an inquisition that left them sad and shaken.

HEARING BOARD MEMBER: I see you have always lived in this country.

NISEI: Yes.

HBM: Are you a dual citizen?

NISEI: No, I am an American citizen only.

HBM: In February, during the army registration, you said "No" to Question 28 according to our record. Did you understand the question?

NISEI: I guess I did understand the question.

HBM: And do you want to change the answer, or do you want the "No" to stand?

NISEI: I'll keep it "No."

HBM: What does that mean?

(The boy stands there. His lips are quivering, but he does not speak.)

HBM: Do you want to talk about it? Something is bothering you?

NISEI: What is bothering me could not be answered by any one person in particular.

HBM: Don't you want to tell us? Perhaps there is something that we can do. If you say "No" you are giving away your American citizenship. Is that what you want to do? Feel free to talk. We're not here to argue with you, but we want to help you.

NISEI: I was thinking . . . that since there is a war on between Japan and America, since the people of this country have to be geared up to fight against Japan, they are taught to hate us. So they don't accept us. First I wanted to help this country, but they evacuated us instead of giving us a chance. Then I wanted to be neutral, but now that you force a decision, I have to say this. We have a Japanese face. Even if I try to be American, I won't be entirely accepted.

HBM: What is this about "the Japanese face" deal? . . . Have you been reading Mary Oyama's article in *Liberty*?

NISEI: I read Mary's article. It doesn't say much. It just tells about the conditions of leaving our homes, about the hardships we suffered and how well we took them. But that was just the

151]

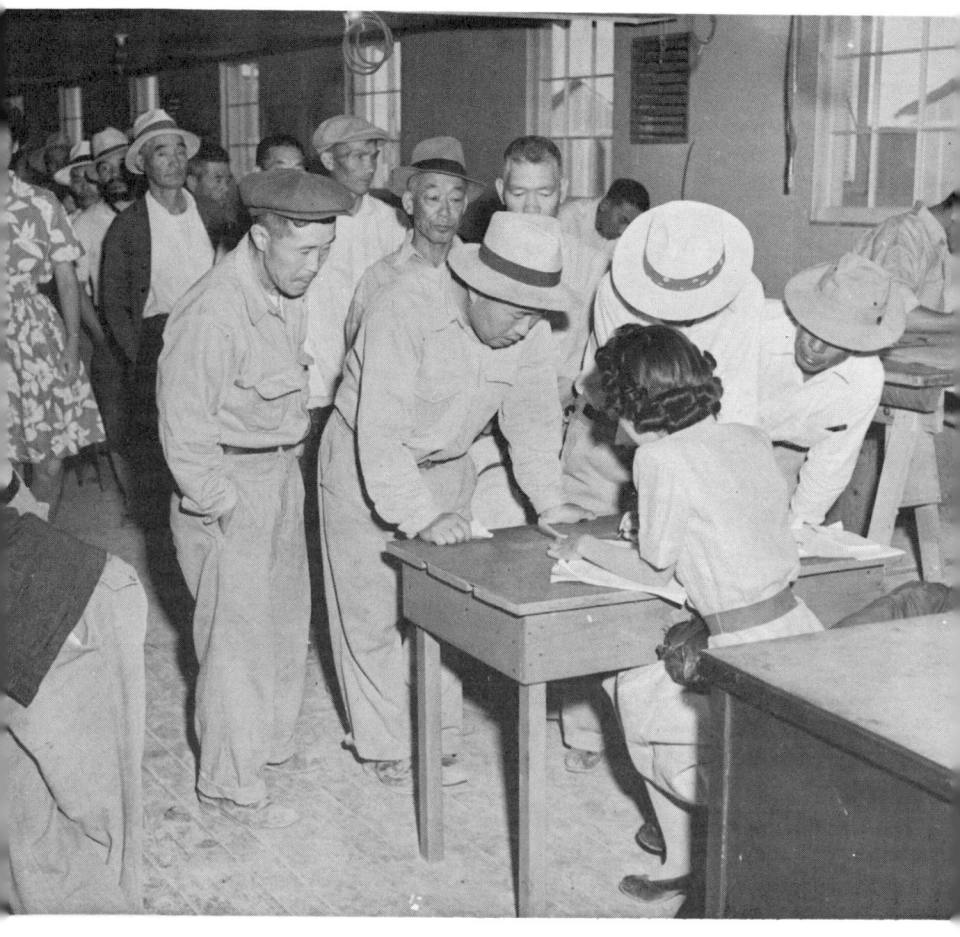

THOSE WHO WANTED REPATRIATION

A number of pro-Japan dissidents, mostly native Isseis, requested a return to Japan, or voluntary removal to the high security center at Tule Lake, in California. Here they are making request for removal from the Poston Center.

—WRA Photo, National Archives.

beginning. A great deal has happened since then that she says nothing about.

HBM: What do you plan to do?

NISEI: I planned to stay in this country before the war . . .

HBM: What about your folks?

NISEI: They'll . . . go to Tule Lake if I do.

HBM: Is it that some of your friends are going to Tule Lake? Are you being influenced by the talk of friends?

NISEI: No, my best friend is going to stay here.

HBM: Then what is at the bottom of this?

NISEI: If I would say "Yes," I'd be expected to say that I'd give up my life for this country. I don't think I could say that because this country has not treated me as a citizen. I could go three-quarters of the way, but not all the way, after what has happened.

HBM: Would you be willing to be drafted?

NISEI: No, I couldn't do that.

HBM: That's all. I see that you have thought about it and that your mind is made up.

(Nisei goes out.)

HBM: I feel sorry for that boy. Some of them I don't feel sorry for.

* * * *

NISEI's later statement to ANALYST:

. . . I thought about this hearing, and how to explain my feelings. But you come before a board like this. I'm not used to it. I couldn't say it the way I meant it. ·

Back home, before the evacuation, when fellows were drafted for the United States Army, that was good. The Japanese gave a party for them, a big sendoff. It was not a party for them all together, but for each one individually. There were fifty people or more at the bus to see each one of them off. You see the white American boys there who were going too. In most cases no one would be there to see them off but the immediate family. We were glad to serve in the American Army then. We thought it was right, because we lived in America.

Before evacuation, all our parents thought that since they were aliens they would probably have to go to a camp. That was only natural—they were enemy aliens. But they never thought that it would

JAPAN BOUND

Crowd assembled at Poston to bid bon voyage to Center residents who left the project by bus and truck August 24, 1943 on the first lap of the journey to Japan via the *Gripsholm*, which sailed from an eastern seaport September 1.

—*Pauline Bates Brown Photo, Poston Collection, University of Arizona.*

come to the place where their sons, who were born in America and who were American citizens would be evacuated . . .

If the American government is honest, if the American people are honest, why don't they investigate what is said before acting? By the time the truth is known, something has been done to us. We never know what is coming next. We have no peace of mind. Every few months it is something else. When we were put here we thought that we'd be here just a few weeks and then would be allowed to go out. When we found out that that wasn't so and that we were all going to be treated like enemy aliens, we thought we would be allowed to stay here in peace as neutrals during the war. We didn't expect all this haggling with the government. We didn't expect that the people would be split and bothered by one request and proposition after another. We didn't expect fights over self-government, registration, volunteering, relocation, and now segregation. Haven't these people been tortured enough? Do you know how many are going to Tule Lake to put an end to this once and for all, to get a little peace of mind?

They talk about relocation now. Do you know that nine-tenths of the people would have relocated themselves without any trouble or much cost to the government if they'd been given a little time and a little help in the beginning? . . .

The FBI picked up all the people who were really dangerous. They ought to have known what they were doing. The humane thing would have been to leave the rest of these people alone. What the old folks really object to is that they spent their whole lives— 30 or 40 years—building up California to what it is today. They don't even care about the fact that they have been kicked around themselves. But when they have built things up to the point where their children can make a living without too much hardship, and then it is all wiped out, it is more than they can take . . .

I don't know Japan. I'm not interested in Japan . . . I don't know what will become of me and people like me if we have to go to Japan. The only thing that might save us is that most of us have our old parents still alive . . . In Japan they respect the old people and, therefore, for their sake they may treat us well . . .

My dad is 58 years old now . . . If I told you the hardships he had, you wouldn't believe me. I owe a lot to my father. Everything I am I owe to him. All through his life he was working for me. During these last years he was happy because he thought he was

155]

coming to the place where his son would have a good life. I am the only son. I have to carry on the family name . . .

I tell you this because it has something to do with my answers about that draft question. We are taught that if you go out to war you should go with the idea that you are never coming back. That's the Japanese way of looking at it. Of course many in the Japanese armies come back after the war, just like in all armies, but the men go out prepared to die. If they live through it, that's their good luck. I listen to American boys talk. They look at it differently . . .

In order to go out prepared and willing to die, expecting to die, you have to believe in what you are fighting for. If I am going to end the family line, if my father is going to lose his only son, it should be for some cause we respect. I believe in democracy, as I was taught in school. I would have been willing to go out forever before evacuation. It's not that I'm a coward or afraid to die. My father would have been willing to see me go out at one time. But my father can't feel the same after this evacuation, and I can't either.

I suppose you know that if there is one thing the Japanese respects, it is integrity. I have to tell the truth. If these questions were just man-to-man talk, it might be all right to say "yes." But if it is to be put down as a record, I want it to be just what I feel. If I feel one per cent different I don't want to say "yes." That's how hard it is for us to answer that question . . .

The Japanese people cannot understand. They were behaving themselves; they were cooperating with others. Yet the American people have turned against them. Even if they were a little different in some ways, there was no cause for it. The people don't understand it. These Japanese would have been the most peaceful group in the country and the most cooperative if they had been left alone instead of being badgered in this way . . .

I thought I would tell some of this to the board. But I have never met people like that before. I can't find the words. They are busy, and have many cases. And so I did just what all the others do—I just gave the surface—not what's deep underneath . . .

I appreciate this talk with you. But my mind is made up. I know my father is planning to return to Japan. I know he expects me to say "No" so there will be no possibility that the family will be separated . . .[2]

[2]"From a Nisei Who Said 'No'," WRA Community Analysis Section, Community Analysis Notes No. 1, Poston Collection, University of Arizona Library. A complete copy of this remarkably candid interview is quoted on pp. 1-8 of that document.

To many an internee it was a sad thing to watch friends and cousins fling away their citizenship. It seemed stark tragedy to watch family-oriented Niseis surrender completely to the plans and dictates of their embittered fathers. As summer weathered in again, it seemed unbelievably odd that one column of the *Chronicle* carried the roll of honor of Poston's inductees into American military service, while opposite was listed the weekly contingent of those willing to forfeit citizenship, and remove themselves to Tule Lake.

To many it was inconsistent and frightening that one bus, loaded with shouting and cheering young men, out to prove their valor, should be followed through the same gates by another bus equally loaded with glum and sad-eyed families headed for Tule. Poston's rebellion had, in the main, been intelligently settled. A better understanding had been gained between management and internees. Progress had been made. Some of the roadblocks had been removed. But everywhere now was a facing up to the enormity of the tragedy that was wringing out the soul of this people.

How could one rationally prove that any young man who followed his father into Tule, who forfeited the citizenship he had been born to, was doing so because of what he called "integrity"? Would anyone believe that a similar young man would choose the other side of the coin for precisely the same reason? How could one make clear this complexity of the Japanese character? Would this riddle remain unfathomed to the end of America's days?

There was this thing called *jicho*. In *jicho* was the key to Japanese behavior. *Jicho* simply meant dignity and self-respect— from parent to child—and from child to parent. Because it remained the compulsive and consistent motivation, there was no real mystery to *nihonjins* why one bus load of Japanese should head for an induction center, and another one to Tule Lake. The pattern of either behavior was understandable.

Their only question was "why must this test be placed so suddenly and so brutally upon our people?" In the naturally

THOSE WHO WOULD NOT CONFORM
Families leaving Poston Center for Tule Lake.

—Poston Collection, courtesy University of Arizona Library.

buoyant Japanese mind there remained the simple conviction that all things must end. Someday this frightening war would be over. Then what of the one hundred and ten thousand homeless Japanese, now housed in ten immense camps? Where would the "yellow peril" *then* go? In spite of setbacks, management was still prating about resettlement. Was there any thought as to how the people might gain back the homes, the farms, the businesses, so suddenly stripped from them? Could they ever hope to *really* win back their standing as citizens?

And, what of those whose hurts, bitterness, and public shame had forced the decision to renounce all? Could they ever, as they hoped, find a new life in a defeated or victorious Japan? Would they someday fight desperately to gain back what they had lost? More important, would America forever hate them?

It took courage for any *nihonjin* to go counter to parental decree and authority. To reject a father's guidance was to reject a father—with a blight of humiliation and dishonor on both parent and child. There were suicides in the camps, and a rash of suicide attempts.

* * * *

"When next I saw Poston, I strutted in wearing a corporal's stripe," Mr. K. reminisces. "We pranced around camp, cocky as hell. All of us considered ourselves as tough little yabos. And the Poston girls sure went for us. I returned to Shelby a married man."

The 442d Regimental Combat Team, out of Shelby, was all Japanese. It was being molded in the same camp, and on the same pattern as had built the tough, gutty, and battle-ready 100th—now furiously fighting in the invasion of Italy. The 442d was a much larger corps than the 100th. It would have to be— from the swelling tide of AJAs coming out of the relocation camps. Japanese Americans were now a little smug in the knowledge their people were delivering superb soldiers to America, and at a most needful time.

Poston's G.I.s, on furlough, talked of and hoped for overseas duty in the Asian phase of the world-wide struggle. All would have willingly fought the nation of their ancestry. But, instead, the 100th was facing Germans and Italians. This could just as likely be the destiny for the 442d.

Everyone smiled a little at the regimental motto for the 442d—"Go For Broke'"—which any camp crapshooter recognized as a favorite phrase for "shoot the works." The fighting 100th, on the other hand, had affectionately called their outfit "One Puka Puka"—Hawaiian pidgin for One Zero Zero.

Over in Asia, American soldiers had quickly recognized the fanatic courage of Japanese fighters. In Italy, the Germans and Italians were facing the same pugnacious adversaries in the little brown men wearing the uniform of the United States. Japanese truly seemed born to the conviction that a man went to war with the expectation of dying. To come back alive was only the slender miracle of fortune. Knowing this, Poston never doubted for a moment but what their young men would bring credit to the camp, and to the nation they fought for.

From the beginning, the war had been a thing of continuing frustration. Now, suddenly, it had moved in close. Loved ones were in jeopardy. Even in Poston, isolated in the Arizona desert, it was now becoming a specter of blood and bayonets.

Through the winter and spring had come a solemn and sobering march of events. First Bizerte had fallen to the Allies; after that Tunis; and then an end to the bloody German resistance in Africa. Almost simultaneously, as the months advanced, had come the sudden and sweeping battle for Italy. AJAs of the 100th were in the blood and mud of the initial invasion. Germany, at last, was feeling the might and determination of America. But she was cutting no blows against England. London already was bombed into shambles, even while American troops invaded the Japanese-held Attu, in the Aleutians. It had been hope and frustration—in equal measure.

And then suddenly Poston sweltered again in the heat of another summer. The great dispersal plan had never gotten off the ground. In spite of heroic effort on the part of Dillon Myer, internees were the same prisoners they had always been. Once more Poston's three great camps were in Arizona's slow bake. The 442d Combat Team had been moved overseas. Now camp letters from "our boys" were being postmarked APO, out of New York.

The *Chronicle* recorded every scrap of news of Poston's soldier boys, and every activity, no matter how small or trivial, of the great triheaded camp it served. What was happening made internees especially proud. What was ahead for these same internees, not even the WRA seemed to know.

TOFU FACTORY, POSTON

Besides making the bean curd *tofu* cakes, these specialists manufactured Poston's *mochigoni*. In *mochigoni,* the heavy rice dough is kneaded and pounded to flaky lightness with beam and paddle, cut into cakes, and deep fried in fat.

—Poston Collection, courtesy University of Arizona Library.

CHAPTER TEN

THE stifling heat of summer was now matched by the oppressive, almost smothering weight of the war. The "under-belly" invasion of Europe had begun at Salerno, and now the press and radio were filled with the merciless and attritious battle for the Messina Straits, to consolidate the Allied toehold on Italy itself. Camp letters were of necessity vague as to where the AJAs were stationed in the battle for Italy, but there could be no doubt now but what Poston's "tough little yabos" were facing guns of the Germans and Italians.

Casualty lists of the boys who had gone out of the camp began to be published and posted. This second hot summer and fall now brought the war more sharply, more terrifyingly close to the internees. Sons of the Poston mothers—brothers to its sisters —husbands to its wives—were fighting in the muck and blood of Italy. But the strange fact was that, in the face of death and sacrifice, the once seething inner rebellion of Poston's residents had evaporated into a grim and expectant calmness.

Gone was the blare of Japanese music, the wavings of hostile flags, the burning of fires, the shouts of the agitators. Present now was an immense and overshadowing pride that the valorous 442d, an AJA army recruited entirely from a displaced and hated minority, had joined the famed 100th in fighting America's battles with a ferocity and courage that was astonishing the world.

163]

Issue after issue of the *Chronicle* listed the names of the recruits still pouring out of Poston, to join the new and impressive fighting units being trained at Shelby. These, complete with Japanese officers, were to serve as endless replacements to the 100th and the 442d.

Out of the pittance pay allowed the employed internees, and out of whatever store of cash they might have salvaged from the expulsion, the three camps of Poston were buying war bonds with a willingness and generosity unmatched in America. Consistently the *Chronicle* mentioned the completion of quota after quota on the bond drives, the generous support of Red Cross and Blood Bank, the almost pathetic eagerness of the internees to prove that they were true Americans.

There was no room now for dissent or rebellion. The Isseis, finally recognized, and given their part in the government of Poston, had subsided into the role of honorable old folks. Most of those with leanings toward Japan had already voluntarily exiled themselves. Now were coming letters from some of them undertoned with uncertainty and a trace of regret for the decisive course they had set. Relatives and friends mourned for them; hoped America would forgive.

The war struggle had become an ever-changing pattern that was reaching across the globe, with its long fingers manipulating even America's lost people in the camps. Naples had fallen to the American armies under General Mark W. Clark, and Poston's boys were in the thick of it. Invaded on her own soil, Italy suddenly and abjectly surrendered—but there was no abject surrender of Germany. Every foot of the way northward was red with the blood of wounded and dying Americans.

With the waning of fall, came winter again on the desert. Came also a widening of the war in the Pacific, with the furious battles for Tarawa and the Makin Islands. Again the winds howled across Poston. Again frost stung and bit at the flesh. But gone were the bonfires. Forgotten were the strikes and the turmoil. And there were stoves, at last, in the barracks.

With winter's establishment of Anzio beach-head in Italy, only twenty-five miles from Rome, Poston was reading that the two AJA armies were now fighting alongside one another. The two all-Japanese units were battling to death and glory in one of the war's most cruel and attritious campaigns. The number of Poston casualties made sick and sad reading. "I got my first one at Suvereto," reminisced Mr. K. "German fire? God, it was awful! The medics told me I was probably out of the war. But I wasn't. They patched me up. They sent me back."

The *Chronicle* carried all the news it could glean concerning the 100th and 442d. There was no question now that the nation at last was cognizant of the worth of its AJA soldiery. Amazing armies had been recruited out of America's feared and rejected citizenry. In battle after battle, these men fought like demons. Already they had become the most decorated units in the history of the United States Army.

There was no denying that the 100th was becoming a legend. Proudly it was being recorded in the press across America—that out of 1300 effective fighters in the 100th, 1000 Purple Hearts had already been awarded, along with 73 Silver Stars, 96 Bronze Stars, 21 Legion of Merit medals, and 16 Division Citations. Every AJA in Italy seemed to be fighting as though life itself depended on it.

The 442d was turning up an equally amazing record.[1] But no matter how proudly recounted were the acclaim and accomplish-

[1]See Orville C. Shirey, *Americans: The Story of the 442d Combat Team.* Washington: Infantry Journal Press, 1946. The record, up to May 1, 1946 was: *Individual Awards*—Medal of Honor, 1; Distinguished Service Cross, 47; Distinguished Service Medal, 1; Oak Leaf Cluster to Silver Star, 12; Silver Star, 342; Legion of Merit, 17; Soldier's Medal, 15; Oak Leaf Cluster to Bronze Star, 38; Bronze Star Medal, 810; Air Medal, 1; Oak Leaf Cluster to Purple Heart Medal, 468; Purple Heart Medal, 2022; Army Commendation, 36; Division Commendation, 87; Croix de Guerre (French), 12; Palm to Croix de Guerre, 2; Croce Al Merito di Guerra (Italian), 2; Medaglia di Bronze al Valor Militaire (Italian), 2. Total number of Individual Awards, 3915. *Unit Awards*—Distinguished Unit Citation, 7; Meritorious Service Unit Plaque, 2; Army Commendation, 1. Total number of Unit Awards, 10.

TOFU FACTORY, POSTON

The native bean curd, *tofu*, is an important and popular part of the Japanese diet. Besides providing the *tofu* for the camp, this busy department also produced *mochigoni*, a leavened and delicate rice cake.

—Poston Collection, courtesy University of Arizona Library.

ments, the story was grim and sad. Every citation, every decoration was inseparably keyed to blood and death. Camp Shelby was kept busy turning out replacements to fill the AJA ranks in Italy.

All of which had forced a change of thinking in California and across America—a reappraisal of the cold and merciless judgment as to the "Japs." A new tone had come into the American press and radio. Magazine articles were now extolling, almost with reverence, the fighting record of the AJAs. Never in history had there been anything to equal the guts and pugnacity of these soldiers. A movie was being planned to record their deeds. Glory was in the air. Forgiveness was in the hearts of men.

And, along with this ground swell of charity, came fresh news out of Washington. Secretary of War Stimson was mellowing. Dillon Myer and John Collier had joined their thinking with Harold Ickes, Secretary of the Interior. At last there was unanimity of opinion—evacuation had been an unnecessary and tragic blunder.

Tardy as was the news, in general, it was good. The record of Japanese Americans in the "loyal" camps had been circumspect and exemplary. A few centers, including Poston and Manzanar, had hosted strikes and rebellions, but after the causes were digested and understood in the top strata of WRA, and made plain at last to the War Department, the apprehensions and worries had evaporated into the new era of trust and good feeling.

The high security camp at Tule Lake now constituted the only real problem in evacuee behavior pattern—and that only because it now housed most of the alien malcontents. By October of 1943 the last contingent of "disloyal" internees had been passed through its gates. On November 1 the camp was shaken by a mass demonstration of protest. Four days later the camp was a scene of riots, and the U. S. Army moved in with machine guns and bayonets. Until the middle of January 1944 the camp was under complete military control.

But even here, as at Poston, the storm eventually died out to a whispering breeze. As Japan's fortunes in war deteriorated against the punishment of America's military might, the vociferous jingoists subsided. A lot of them, now, were less than sure they wanted eventual repatriation. Many of Tule's internees were having second thoughts about their hasty renunciation of American citizenship.

In the nine other great centers, all was serenity and accommodation. On January 20, Secretary of War Stimson, as a sort of inept compliment to AJA loyalty and trustworthiness, publicly extended the military draft to *all* Japanese Americans. If they were safe enough to be drafted, they were safe enough for anything.

But in midst of all the good feeling and joy, the greatest crisis for Poston was gathering—as it was gathering for the internees of every other relocation camp in the nation. Before this strange year closed itself out, the War Department announced that, effective on January 2, the bitter and hateful exclusion orders against the Japanese would be revoked. And, after the Supreme Court handed down the rulings which challenged America's right to incarcerate 110,000 members of its citizenry, Dillon Myer announced that all relocation centers would be phased out before the end of 1945. By June 30, 1946, the entire War Relocation Authority program was to be scrapped and liquidated.

In essence, it was official pronouncement to the Japanese that soon they would be free to go home. But with their homes gone, their businesses vanished, with families divided and destroyed, every internee knew that the going home was likely to be a hell of a lot worse than the going away.

Every hint of dispersion of Poston's internees now brought shudders of apprehension. Everyone wanted to go home, of course. But not for a fraction of these people could there *ever* be a return home. The exigencies of war, and the greed of men, had devoured their birthright. Should the government tender even partial recompense for Japanese losses—of which there was some talk and less promise—the present owners of California's immense dowry would never readily or graciously yield up their windfall.

The shops were either vandalized, vanished, or operated by other enterprising opportunists. California's once great spread of Japanese farms, truck gardens, and floral husbandry, was being profitably operated by those who had moved into the big roust's sudden vacuum. It was plain now that nothing could ever be regained without a fight.

Never could there be a return to Terminal Island. Fish Harbor's canneries still operated—now manned by Italians and Slavs —but the Japanese dwellings had been leveled, and bulldozed away. Few people, other than Naval, customs, and prison personnel, now slept on Terminal Island. The fishing boats had been confiscated; the tuna fleet would never again be Japanese-operated. Fish Harbor's residents must, of necessity, seek another place in the world.

New and frightening edicts continued to plunge the ten great camps ever deeper into worry and gloom. In the meantime, while they coped with the imponderables, the internees must somehow carry on. Casualty lists, camp funerals, enlistments, pompous government declarations, and the course of the war, were the sober and somber notes that weighted the *Chronicle's* pages. Even in this little paper, it was a constant challenge to strive for the light touch.

By generous doling out of bylines, the paper had a reporter in every block in all three of Poston's camps. Parties, marriages, childbirths were endlessly chronicled, along with the usual small-town personal trivia. But this was the grist that kept its little crew busy at the typing and stenciling machines.

A sort of lexicon of center talk was kept going issue after issue, not only in the *Chronicle,* but in other relocation media. All it consisted of was a glossary of commonly used words—half English—half Japanese—but wholly camp. *Ponkin*—was camp for "pumpkin," usually as "pumpkin head;" *bon hedo*—a bone head; *basuketto buro*—basketball; *sofuto boru*—softball; *mesu harr*—

SCENE: A barron and dust-covered barrack. In the center were found two empty barrels, bridged by a wooden board. A single typewriter, so out of place yet so nobly, rested upon the supported plank.

It was here that on May 12, when Poston had only a handful much ado.

The Blk. mgrs. in return acted as guardians of the fourth estate for they contributed their share in the making of the daily bulletin, with reports of Lost and Found articles, and minor announcements. Between them and the Administration, the

OFFICIAL INFORMATION BULLETIN

Relocation Center - Poston, Arizona

VOL. 1	Wednesday, May 13, 1942	NO..

**** ***
‡ IMPORTANT! FURNITURE MOVEMENT

Several persons have inquired about having their household furniture and personal effects transported to Poston. Under instructions which we have received, an~pers~can~h~his personal pro~ty tran~

of evacuees, Misses Ruth Ogawa and Marie Doi reported to work on a rushed assignment, to begin a Community newspaper.

Thanks to the typewriter, a ream of paper, and some carbon sheets, the first 60 copies of the note-book sized official Bulletin, Vol. 1 No. 1 made its meek appearance the next day. The new-born editions were then sent to Every Ad. office and the Block Manager's office with vernacular sheet survived on of the "stormiest" days in now, gathering feats, facing handicaps before unknown.

On May 22, nine days after birth, today's newly named an popularly known as the Daily Poston Chronicle, donned it new dress by coming out in mi meograph style. It was reall quite a 'jump' then, markin its progress---Vol. 1 No. 9.

MASTHEAD OF THE POSTON CHRONICLE
This reproduction of the masthead of Poston's little mimeographed newspaper appeared in *Poston Notes and Activities*, compiled and edited by Henry Mori.

—Courtesy Henry Mori.

mess hall; *bata*—butter; *buroni*—bologna; *egisu*—eggs; *weini*—weiners; *supu* — soup; *rosu* — roast; *baketsu* — bucket; *bottoru* — bottle; *buraku*—block.

Americanese became picturesque when worke(through either Japanese humor or Japanese auditory shortcou..ngs. A *block head* became the accepted term for block manager, and often in a derogatory way. *Poston tuxedo* was another name for the bib overalls furnished the workers in either agriculture or mechanics. The *moving and hauling company* was the division or relocation office. And *daikon legs* was applied to the legs of some Japanese girls, simply because they had resemblance to the shapeless radish used in Japanese pickling. *Orri* became the contraction for "all right;" *penki* was "paint;" *koppu* meant "cup;" and *pow* was the unmistakable term for "finished."

Those who excelled at handcrafts got special mention. The artists, the actors, the singers were recognized publicly in print. The poets and essayists were given a little too much space in the columns.

The baseball stars, the judo and sumo experts, and the diving and boxing idols were seldom neglected. Interviewed were the oddballs, the recalcitrants, the aimless or vociferous, as they wandered through camp. Occasionally the *Chronicle* talked about the big subsistence trucks that rolled into Parker where, at the railroad terminal, they loaded the supplies so vital to the existence of the triheaded Poston.

In a little newspaper, cut to paucity by lack of production equipment, bedeviled by wartime scarcities, and under the hard heel of camp management, there was never enough space to talk of worthier things. For instance, it seldom mentioned the incredible and instinctual adaptability of the Japanese race.

Most internees had to cross the canal to go to and from work. The twelve-dollar-a-month workmen might be ordered, by management, to span the canal, at some particular point, with a foot bridge. All they had to work with would be the timbers and scrap lumber from Poston's discard piles. But, using the most unpromising materials, coupled with innate artistry, they some-

171]

how would delicately fashion a bridge worthy of any water garden in the Old Country.

Far down the canal, toward one of the swimming basins, other Japanese workmen had lugged tons of rock from the foothills and, with impeccable taste, had laid them up into patterns of great beauty. It seemed impossible for a Japanese laborer to plan even a vegetable garden without utilizing taste and symmetry. Under this compulsion to refine and beautify, even ugly old Poston was slowly emerging in little patterns of sightly loveliness.

The Japanese mind seemed to abhor and reject ugliness in any form. Whatever a *nihonjin* touched, he somehow improved. And, there were internees whose thinking turned to philosophy. There were those who reasoned that if their people could seek such peace and beautification in this evil place, surely, somehow, they would respectfully, and with dignity, come out of their present travail.

In compliance with that native instinct for silence regarding news which could not be uttered with honor, there came little public mention of the uglier aspects of Poston. Despair and incarceration had bred more than its logical share of drunkenness, abetted by the whiskey bootlegged into camp by the liquor entrepreneurs at Parker and Yuma. Gambling, always endemic with Japanese, had become a way of life to many an internee.

But worst was the discernible breakdown in morals of the most moralistic people on earth. Close confinement of the thousands of young people had brought its inevitable results. Marriages were not quite catching up with the births. And, among one's people, it was neither mete nor proper to take public notice of the unwed mothers and their babies, of which the hospital was an important ministry.

To the unsung journalists of Poston should go the greater credit for this new era of tranquility and good feeling. With their battered typewriters, ridiculously inadequate publishing equipment, and tireless energy, they served up to the camp its daily grist of news and comment. This task was never easy; and seldom appreciated. Poston, at this time, was third largest city in Arizona. Without linotypes, without printing presses, and with only half-hearted backing and support from management, their mimeographed *Chronicle* was the only public voice the people possessed.

On September 1, 1942, the *Chronicle* celebrated its one-hundredth edition by laying the cornerstone to its own projected building. The new adobe quarters, when built, would mean the hoped-for escape from windblown dust and filth of the tar-papered shack in which the *Press-Bulletin,* its predecessor, had been born—the humble little sheet that had metamorphosed into the still humble *Chronicle.* Into the building's cornerstone were inserted copies of this hundredth issue. The stone, designed and fashioned by Mitchell Nakagawa, was duly cemented over--to become a corner of another Poston I "permanent" building. Present at the dedication had been Director Wade Head, and the *hakujin* press supervisor, Norris E. James.

It was months after the "uprising" before the building was far enough along for the staff to move typewriters and mimeographs into the clean new quarters. By then each of the three camps comprising Poston was represented by a "city editor." Susumu Matsumoto screened and funneled the news for Unit 1; Kaz Oka and Yoshiye Takata shared desk for Unit 2; Isao Fukuba and Margaret Hirashima jointly served Unit 3. Heading the overall staff, and working as camp twelve-dollar-a-month "leg men" were former reporters out of California's once famed Japanese dailies. Some very excellent artists willingly served the little sheet with sketches and cartoons.

Their work in telling the inside story of Poston was not entirely confined to the daily effusion from the camp's rickety mimeographs. Henry Mori—later respected editor of the English section of the Los Angeles daily *Rafu Shimpo*—found himself, as a young reporter, incarcerated at Poston, and a part of the *Chronicle* crew. But, more than that, it was Henry Mori who promoted and produced *Poston Notes and Activities,* a magazine spawned under the most adverse conditions imaginable.

Assisting in this ambitious endeavor was Kenny Hirose, the *Chronicle's* promotional advertising manager, and staff artists George Okamoto, Janet Tateishi, and Wakako Nakamura. Management's Karl Dike served as map draftsman. Ruth Ogawa, Mariko Matsumoto, and Mariko Komatsuka were the publication's willing and essential stencil cutters. But in a concentration camp, regardless of devotion and talent, even a magazine had to come out as a mimeographed package.

Poston Notes and Activities made its appearance April 1943. Amazingly, it carried advertising from Phoenix and New York (mimeographed), and a full-page stenciled ad from Sears Roebuck. More than that, it boasted pages devoted to activities at the far-away camps of Manzanar, Tule Lake, Gila River, Heart Mountain, Minidoka, Granada, Topaz, Rohwer, and Jerome. Most of its seventy-six pages, however, were crammed with the reflective heartbeat of Poston.

"We had a most trying and difficult time getting it out," says editor Henry Mori. "We had planned *Poston Notes and Activities* for the beginning of the year 1943. It was April before we could get it into covers. And we peddled it for a dime a copy. I'm sure collectc ; are paying more than a dime a copy for it today.

"To get our publication out, we had to plead for paper. To print it, we had to borrow the mimeograph machine from Poston I Red Cross. No periodical ever was born under more discouraging circumstances. And no publication died more quickly."

There was a lot to know about the underbelly of Poston. Much of what they knew, the camp journalists could never record. But in spite of every handicap and discouragement, the mirror they held up to their people was steamy with the lifebreath of their immense prison.

Could management have more assiduously curtailed their "policy" handouts in favor of the common tone of joys and trials, and had the War Relocation Authority, or some governmental agency, granted these dedicated craftsmen the printing equipment so desperately needed to cope with stark necessity, Poston might have been more adequately served. The great triheaded camp deserved better. Poston's journalists—along with most of Poston's internees—knew far more about their city in the sun than all the booted and hatted camp bosses, and all the stress experts the government had assembled to study it.

LAST OF THE INTERNEES LEAVE POSTON
In 1945 the final contingents of Japanese Americans take leave of Poston
Relocation Camp, where they have lived for three eventful years.

—WRA Photo, National Archives.

CHAPTER ELEVEN

THROUGH winter and spring, around the world, it was battle and carnage. The war had erupted into death and destruction unequaled in all of history. In lost and forgotten Poston were being published lists of casualties that were frightening and sobering. These were boys out of camp. The war was hitting fearfully close.

It was curious how the internees watched and listened to the news regarding the ancient homeland. For by now America's military pressure had forced Premier Tojo to inform the Japanese Diet that the war situation was "truly grave." The Solomons and Hollandia had fallen to American victory, and the Burmese campaign had exploded into new fury. Plight of their ancestral nation drew passing interest, but it was news out of Italy that rated the real concern.

In rapid succession came reports of the fall af Cassino, and the eruptive fury of the Anzio wedge aimed at Rome. Then Rome fell to the fighting Americans, and the next day came announcement of the great Allied invasion of Europe. It was a time of wait and worry.

While the bestial struggle for Europe went on, north and south, the first flying bombs began dropping on England. And Japan proper got its raking of American fire and explosives from the air. Then the forces of Admiral Nimitz landed on Saipan, followed by the Battle of the Philippine Sea. Japan at last was writhing under the squeeze of the pincers.

At Tule Lake—sulking, hurt, oftentimes uncommunicative—were the recalcitrant families who had voluntarily exiled themselves from Poston and other relocation camps. Across the world, slogging their way through Italy, were the AJAs who had just as quickly responded in another area of choice. To those in the camps poignantly concerned with the war effort—those who waited and worried—it was disquieting to know that not even membership in the most valorous and decorated units in the American Army was insurance against enemy bullets and shrapnel. Many an anxiety-ridden internee had come to the conclusion, after scanning the weekly casualties, that the AJAs were getting a lot more than their share of death's exposure to the enemy. Some were of the opinion that, just because they were Japanese, they were expendable.

The telegrams that came into Poston were terse. They were grudging in their words. To those who received them, it was as though the government had striven to save pennies by the brevity of the message. Private —— had died in action, while serving with the 442d, Fifth Army, Italian Campaign. Exactly when, or how, was invariably left to conjecture.

On the other hand, many a Poston boy, as a fighting member of the renowned all-Japanese battalions that were startling the world, had survived the throb and struggle of the push up the boot toward Rome. He had lived through the bitterly contested landing at Anzio, and the seesaw battles across the Volturno River. He had shared the bloody struggle out of the Anzio wedge, and on into Rome.

He had seen the "eternal city." He had slogged past the Colosseum, squinted a sleepy eye at Hadrian's Tomb, and had gazed on the dome of St. Peter's at a distance. Rome's weather, he had discovered, was hot; drippy like a *furo* bath. None of the cooling fog, like at Terminal Island, or the truck garden areas along the California coast. The war was over for the Italians; they had thrown in the sponge. They veed their fingers for victory. They loved and coddled the weary AJAs, in hopes of scrounging cigarettes or chocolate. But the Germans were not nearly so loving. After Rome, it was one continuous grind at them again—in the mountains and valleys northward. For AJAs, it was one hell of a hard and awful war.

On the 25th of July, the battered and decimated 100th was pulled out of the line at Pontedera, moved down from Leghorn, and trucked south to Vada—the 34th Division rest center on the Italian coast, and only a few miles north of Cecina. It was there they joined the equally punch-drunk 442d Combat Team for the pause which the AJAs had thought would never come, and for which every buddhahead and kotonk had prayed through the seemingly endless punishment of months past.

It was good. Vada proved by far the best rest camp they had known since that far day when they had crossed the Messina Straits to Salerno. Some were allowed to drop their bedrolls in those crazy little wooden bath cottages which still dotted the Italian beach front like a redding case of acne. Others just tented, or laid the beaches alongside their slit trenches. The cottages were scarcely big enough for even the bedsack of a short man, but their unpainted inner walls were enriched with penciled initials, sensual notes, and the phallic symbols drawn by eager Italian girls in those peaceful years before the war.

Never had the men felt so physically depleted. Vada was another name for rest. They might get an occasional air raid, but, by now, the weary young men would never have traded a wink of slumber to run for a slit trench. The red cottages so far had fared well in the war. The Jerries seemed to have chosen better targets than beach huts for their scarce and expensive bombs. Rest was gratefully taken when one got it. There was constant danger of it being cut short.

Here at Vada, as always, would come retraining for the veterans, and battle drill for the replacements. The new boys, so continuously drawn from Shelby, would learn fast from their battle-wise and hardened mentors. Here at last, at Vada, were movies, swimming, ample and edible food, and a USO outfit that was going all out to make them forget the misery and carnage. Here performers could perform, without the front-line risk of getting shot at, or having their show trucks blown to confetti by one of the cleverly planted German mines.

To the kotonks out of California, the seacoast of Italy, and the climate, reminded nostalgically of home. Here one heard the pound of the surf, the squawk of the gulls, and the war seemed far away. To the buddhaheads out of warm and salubrious Hawaii, it was equally meaningful and comforting.

It seemed such a far day, so dim and distant to recollection, when the 100th had first faced up to this grim and brutal struggle. Oran had been a mud and brick cesspool of filth and stench. Its docks, streets and mud buildings had been torn to hell in the initial African invasion, but by the time their own tired convoy had put into its bay, and the *James Parker* had spewed out its enervated and seasick AJAs, Oran had once again returned to its century-old normalcy. Its populace, draped in their lice-ridden shrouds of unwashed cotton, had moved back to their dark and sinuous quarters without ever bothering to patch up the war holes.

From Oran the grinding, whining trucks had hauled the AJAs through the choking dust, inland to Fleurus—past the rolling hills of wheat fields, the moisture-collecting valleys green with vineyards and citrus. This certainly was not England, where the AJAs had expected the ship convoy was taking them. But, surprise or not, the land—any land—looked good after the cramped weeks between rusting ship hull plates, as the vessel had inched its way across the Atlantic's rough and uneasy waters.

The *James Parker*, a former banana boat in the South American trade run, had taken them aboard at a Staten Island dock. And, while the other ships of the convoy were tediously gathered from the tentacles of New York and Jersey harbors, the men had tried to accustom themselves to living aboard her. That, no one had quite been able to do. For kotonks, this was the first voyage. For the buddhaheads, out of Hawaii, it was their second sea trip.

When finally the convoy had put through the Straits of Gibraltar, and it had dawned on the travelers that their destination would be in the fighting area of North Africa, instead of

England, the men had grown nervous and worried. But they had entered Oran without firing a shot. Brave men before them had done the fighting, and had secured the coast for landings. They had been greeted in Oran's narrow streets by the donkeys, goats, and sheet-draped beggars who slept with their animals in these same stench-ridden streets and gutters. The better-heeled populace, already wearied of greeting Allied soldiery, had never even bothered to raise salutation's hand to the strange little army that had come off the *Parker.*

What greetings there were had come from the wheedling "sheiks," selling wire jewelry and pornographic photos. While the men had waited for the motor convoy to take them inland, the more serious merchandising had been done by dozens of little Arab boys on the hustle. Unblushingly they had praised the sexual accomplishments of their "beeg sisters," their little faces turned up imploringly. For one American two-bit piece they would take the soldier to their "beeg sister." For one American dollar the whole deal could be consummated.

It was good that the motor convoy had hurried the 100th out of Oran without too much contamination. But Fleurus had proven another stinking hive of mud cells and decay. Their camp, a few miles removed, had been the staging area of Goat Hill. And Goat Hill had the more familiar American smell.

Other Army units had used the hill, and had gone on to the battle grounds of North Africa. Its previous occupants had given the bivouac its name. And what they thought about it was volubly inscribed on the walls of its wooden sheds and latrines.

The commanding officers, Colonels Farrant L. Turner and James W. Lovell, with their aides, had been taken off by jeep to the Mediterranean Base Section headquarters at Oran. While the men groused and battle-drilled at Goat Hill, their officers were being briefed on what the future held for the 100th in this war. Two days later Turner and Lovell were back at Goat Hill, dourly confirming the rumors that the proud 100th's future was to hunt thieves in the Algerian desert. The natives were stealing and grafting themselves into wealth. The guilty ones must be apprehended and militarily punished. To AJAs, chafingly anxious to prove themselves against a more logical enemy, there was deep resentment at this betrayal.

Then, while men and officers were trying to digest this really bad news, a command car had arrived at the Goat Hill bivouac, and Turner had been whisked away to Fifth Army headquarters, at Mastaganuna. Next day Turner was back at Goat Hill. This time the colonel wore an amiable grin on his tanned and weathered cheeks. This time the news was better. To the high command, Turner had done a first class job of selling his tough and beloved little yabos.

The 100th was to be assigned to the 34th Division — the famous Red Bulls.[1] Tomorrow a motor convoy would take the whole Battalion to the 34th's bivouac, back at Oran.

In the States, the 34th had, like the AJAs' own, started out as a National Guard outfit. The Red Bulls, manned by big Swedes and Poles from Iowa, Minnesota, the Dakotas, and Nebraska, had been the first American division to hit Europe after the war started. It had trained in North Ireland, and had seen plenty of action. They had shared a big part in the invasion of North Africa, and had taken a brutal mauling at Kasserine—where their 168th Regiment was almost totally destroyed. But the 34th had come through, had stormed Hill 609, and had knocked out every German defense assigned them before Tunis. Now they were licking wounds outside Oran; getting their replacements; preparing to fight again.

The Red Bulls had paid blood for the right to be called veterans. Their casualties had been murderously heavy—4,254 men killed, wounded and missing—more than a third of this division's original effective. The 100th was to replace their 2d Battalion of the 133d Regiment. The 2d Battalion had been assigned as special military guard to General Eisenhower's headquarters in Algiers. It was understandable that, at first, the big men of the Red Bulls had been only vaguely impressed by the runt-sized

[1]See Thomas D. Murphy, *Ambassadors In Arms,* The Story of the 100th Battalion, p. 120.

men of the 100th. But the AJAs were proud and happy about their assignment.

The hundred-acre bivouac of the 34th Division was centered in a forest of cork trees, a few miles outside Oran. When the trucks of the long convoy had pulled into the parade grounds, the AJAs, as they clambered out of the tail-gates into formation, had been greeted by the music of the 133d Infantry band. By the time the 100th's own band could strike out music at head of its own column, its staff officers had shaken hands with Colonel Ray C. Fountain.

The tall and burly veterans of the battlewise 34th had dourly appraised the fifteen hundred little brown soldiers. There had been smiles—even contempt—but it had been the supercilious attitude of any veteran at sight of an unpromising rookie. The big Swedes from America's midwest could not help but eye the Japanese with smug derision—but in their looks was none of the hysteric hate of California, and none of the racial animosity the AJAs had known so long in Mississippi and their final camp in Louisiana. The Red Bulls had confronted their new buddies with the same "show me, Bub" attitude the buddhaheads had met in Wisconsin.

Willingly and gleefully the AJAs had sewn on their Red Bull shoulder patches. By nightfall the more curious and amiable of the Red Bulls were drifting over to the 100th's tented area. Soon they were singing Hawaiian songs with the buddhaheads, and sharing enough Algerian wine to cement the bonds of friendship.

The AJAs, without fuss or complaint, had knuckled down to the long and grueling battle practice which, for many weeks, was poured upon them. Company by company they had been schooled by veterans of the Tunisian campaign, in everything they knew about Jerry's bag of tricks. In Oran had come the toughest drill, and the most exhaustive training the AJAs had yet encountered. Grimly now, every man had known they were being hardened and seasoned to face the enemy.

Where they would draw battle had been sheer speculation. There was still a lot of war to be fought in North Africa. There were predictions and rumors that the invasion of Italy, or southern France, was imminent. Certainly this battle practice had deep and pregnant meaning. But to these soldiers—every Japanese GI—even Oran looked sweeter now that they could face the world, head high, as honest to God American fighting men. Oran was not California or Hawaii. But for the 100th, in this war, it had been the best yet.

No battle unit could ever have gotten closer to war's fundamentals than had the 100th. After Oran it was nothing but strife and blood—Africa, then across the Mediterranean to Salerno, then north, through Rome, to Leghorn—every step of the way paid out in toil and gore. The bivouac at Vada was a time only for the battle-weary unit to catch its breath.

The next day after the Vada arrival, the Island boys of the 100th took the best and surest way to relax and forget their miseries, by treating themselves to *kalua* pig (pit roasted), and by inviting their grinning and gesticulating Italian village neighbors to share their beach *luaua*. That the Italians were feasting on their own pigs would dawn on them in a few days, with the usual appeal to the officers for tardy payment. The boys of the 100th were resourceful scroungers.

Once again the music had broken out. The Italians liked that. Most of the ukeleles and guitars had long ago been blown into never never land, but vocally the men made up for it in the pure joy of rest and freedom. And the Italian villagers, on their own strings and accordions learned fast to adapt the Latin beat to the island songs.

And in this great and historic pause at Vada, the men were actually being issued travel passes to the conquered cities and towns as far south as Rome. They had earned them. The buoyant and cheerful AJAs here, as always, were finding no trouble at all in getting along with the pitifully despoiled Italian populace.

But the Vada idyll was, as usual, soon broken. The 34th Division headquarters had been notified that General Mark Clark was on his way from Rome, for the prestigious purpose of

[184

reviewing the AJAs, to again personally commend and cite the men, and to honor the 100th with the coveted Distinguished Unit Citation.

So, three days after tasting the luxury of the Vada billet, the 100th was dressed out in new and clean uniforms. And on the 34th's parade grounds, on the highlands above the beach, the regiment stood at attention to receive its honors. It was a damp and murky morning, like Long Beach or San Pedro before the sun completely burned away the haze and fog. The men stood while General Clark personally tied the blue streamers of the citation to the battalion's colors, and pinned on the survivors of the Battle of Belvedere and many another close waltz with the Jerries, the individual badges and ribbons for heroism and battle wounds.

Those who felt the General's fingers as he pinned the Silver Star or less on their pocket flaps were not thinking too much on personal pride. Their thoughts were more likely on the many little brown faces they never again would see. Only the lucky ones were in these lines.

The moment of greater pride came later, when Clark closed the honor review with a brief speech that touched the heart and conscience of every man standing stiffly attentive. There was no question about what the men were thinking—of loved ones under the ban—unproven in Hawaii—incarcerated in America. To the AJAs, the General's words were sweet only because they were proof of effort, and vindication.

It was a short panegyric—the kind of speech every man could accept and digest. But, if only Mark Clark could have added that "You have done enough—now you're going home," the AJAs would have been forever satisfied.

Vada must serve as next best thing. But in military life, a rest camp was too often misnamed. Vada proved no exception. For, on the very morning after Clark's ceremony, the 100th was serving as a guard of honor for another spit-and-polish review—staged this day for King George VI of England, the commander of the U. S. Army Service Forces, and the American Undersecretary of War.[2]

Next morning, Companies A and B were trucked to Leghorn for turns of guard duty in the shattered and beleagured city, and then back to Vada, to share the 100th's memorial service for its dead.[3]

This time many a man shut his eyes in tears as the little army stood at attention, on the parade ground, while the band played softly, and the names were called—one by one. These were the boys who had perished through the endless months of slogging northward in the face of a determined foe who exacted blood-and-death payment for every yard of ground gained. To the living, it seemed that the call-out of names would never end. Two-thirds of the present 100th were AJA replacements, ground out at the Shelby mill. Less than one out of three were left from the original corps that had marched off the *James Parker* at Oran.

To the men of the 100th, it seemed that the Fifth Army high command had sadistically measured their Vada days of rest, thought and glory, before the final knock-over. Scarcely had the men digested the memorial service when, the next day, came news of the latest brasshead machination against brave and willing men. After all the sacrifice—after all the glory—after all the valor expended to make the 100th unique, distinguished, even revered—it had all come to naught.

At Vada, the 100th Battalion (separate corps), was now redesignated by the high command as the 100th Battalion, 442d Regiment. There were howls of protest from the men. There was resentment, and discouragement. The big gripe was that the 100th had pioneered the whole concept of AJAs in the role of a separate fighting unit.

Their eagerness and adaptivity, beginning at Camp McCoy in Wisconsin, through Camps Shelby in Mississippi, and Claibourne in Louisiana, on into the cruel fighting in Italy, had

[2]See Thomas D. Murphy, *Ambassadors In Arms,* The Story of the 100th Battalion, p. 219.
[3]*Ibid.,* p. 219.

pointed the way for Japanese Americans to prove themselves. Their unsurpassed battle record, their unparalleled guts and courage, had shown to all the world that the AJA was a soldier. The 100th had laid the mold, and marked the path for the 442d. And the 442d had followed sedulously in their footsteps. What could not be denied was that the 442d was a bigger army, and once under fire, had proven itself a superb one. But the men were asking—why the 100th—unique, and understandably proud—must be merged into the force for which it had served as guide and mentor?

From Shelby, all the 442d had done for the 100th was to furnish replacements as the casualties piled up. None of the wily veterans of the 100th had ever been tendered officerial posts in the later-formed 442d. No commands had been dished out to the old-hands—in the organization and training of the new corps. Battle weary AJA officers were remembering bitterly that it was the other way about. "Ninety-day wonders," fresh from the States, had been sent over to lead into action men already seasoned by endless confrontations with the enemy. The men of the 100th had died as though the high command considered them deliberate expendables. Now the stepson was taking over. Now came the merging. Now came the loss of identity.

The enemy, they had been informed, was in "strategic retreat," but the Jerries were ever the specialists at making men pay for barking at their tail. It was at Chuisano that the 100th had suffered its first casualties, and spawned its first hero. Shigeo Takata had walked directly into a Jerry nest. Takata had continued to fire his automatic rifle, until he was cut down. Dying, he had been able to tell where the German gunners were—but another AJA was killed, and seven more wounded, before that nest was taken.[4]

Who could forget the waist-deep fighting in the Volturno River, and the struggle toward San Angelo—five days to move seven miles? By November the 100th had occupied Cicilano,

[4]*Ibid.*, p. 128.

only to face another endless struggle for the mined and nested hills of Italy.

Even in retrospect it was a bad dream. Because, to capture Rome, the German winter line had to be knocked out. And German heavy defenses blocked every gate to the Liri Valley. One remembered the little things, like that day after Thanksgiving, when the 100th had gotten its tardy issue of cold turkey, mule-packed up the mountain trails. The white meat had grown a little green and hairy by the journey. By that time the men were getting accustomed to designation of hills by numbers. No man ever grew accustomed to the price one paid to wrest those hills from the enemy.

January had found the 100th dug in at Cassino—facing the Gustav line—the line which Hitler had ordered his Todt organization to build as impregnable. Who could forget the heartbreak of Castle and Monastery Hills? Americans and British, with everything they possessed, had failed at cracking the Gustav.

Eventually the Allies had accomplished the miracle, not by hammering through the line, but by striking behind it—with the surprise amphibious beach landing at Anzio. Grimly, until March, these gutty invaders of the VI Corps had held on while the Germans launched attack after attack on their battered positions. No question but what Anzio had proven costly—but when the Germans finally realized they were not going to push the invaders into the sea, they had been forced again to the defensive. The 100th had been pulled out of their mountain fox holes, and had been shipped by LSTs from Naples to the hard-won Anzio wedge.

Who could forget the murderous fire at Pian Marano and Lanuvio—when six men won DSCs, and the casualties had made one's flesh creep? Three days later the AJAs had fought their way ten miles beyond Valleranello, and the Germans at last were in full retreat. Just another ten miles, and the 100th could have been the first Allied troops to enter Rome. But some brasshead had stupidly given the order for them to await motor transportation for the entry. They had been forced to tarry at roadside, weary and heartbroken, while half the units in Italy streaked past—Rome bound—on Highways 6 and 7.[5]

By the time their tardy motor convoy had finally gotten them into the Eternal City, the cheers and the big party were over. Romans had grown weary of waving at the Allied victors. All was quiet, all was routine, when the haggard Japanese made their belated entry.

But that other rest pause at Civitavecchia, forty miles above Rome, had been as sweet and meaningful as Vada. It hadn't been all rest, of course; these things never were. There were replacements from Shelby to be trained; new weaponry to be mastered. But it was here at Civitavecchia that the 442d Combat Unit, the greater AJA army that had followed the 100th out of Shelby and into the bitter fighting in Italy, had been moved into bivouac alongside. Between the buddhaheads and the kotonks there had been fraternization and fights. Movies and swims. Trips to Rome—and plenty of bragging from both sides. Out of the Civitavecchia bivouac had probably spawned that ignominious general order that was now attaching the 100th to its own child of war—the 442d.

And then had come an end to Rome and Civitavecchia. And then had come Belvedere. And then had come the Arno. Only six days after Rome, they all were again in combat. Through mine fields and merciless mortar and machine gun fire they had moved on again to Suvereto to again try to flank Belvedere from the east and north. The Germans had been well dug in on the heights. The fighting had tested the best of the veterans. It had scared hell out of the Shelby replacements.

And it was at Belvedere that the little yellow-bellies had finally met the enemy squarely—and had taken his measure. On the 26th and 27th of June they had torn the guts out of the Germans; had opened a hole in that impregnable defense wide enough for hell itself to drive through. It was in the din and fury of Belve-

[5] *Ibid.*, p. 190.

dere that the 100th had won the Presidential Citation. The price they had paid for Belvedere had been sufficient to bring Mark Clark to Vada to pin on the ribbons.

And now this last humiliation and sorrow—that the gutty and pugnacious 100th was to be swallowed up, to lose its identity, in union with the 442d. In marriage, it was the bride who surrendered the name. The 100th had become the distaff side of the joir

To anyone but an AJA the gabble and grousing of the men over the merging of the two units would have made little sense. There was hesitance and outright refusal of the Island boys to tear off their Red Bull shoulder patches of the 34th Division in favor of the new patches unique to the union of the AJAs. To hear the vocal fury, one might have thought the war was a grudge fight between the buddhaheads and the kotonks. But to the AJAs at Vada, the war was a lot more. A lot more.

Now it was by truck, forty miles south, to Piombino—for embarkation. And it was the luck of the 100th Battalion of the 442d Regiment to draw the *John Holmes*—with·two latrines for more than one thousand passengers—for the voyage back to Naples. The newly aligned unit drew 181 replacements from Shelby, to fill out its decimated ranks.

Three busy weeks at the staging area in Bagnoli—while they taught the rookies how to duck-waltz through German mine fields and machine gun nests. Then suddenly the whole outfit was aboard the *U.S.S. Samuel Chase*, bound for Marseille, in France. For the AJAs, at last, the war was heading them into the heartland of the enemy. Most of the men were grimly convinced they were expendables. As usual, they were being sent where the war was.

From Marseille it was four hundred miles up the Rhone Valley, by motor convoy, to the dug-in Germans in the Vosge Mountains. Someone must have sensed and anticipated the mess they were facing, because here, for this assault, they were given the help of Company C, 636th Tank Destroyer Battalion; Company

D, 83d Chemical Mortar Battalion; and the tanks of Company B, 752d Tank Battalion.[6]

Once again they met the enemy in the mountains—pine-clad this time—and in almost constant rain. Here the AJAs painfully learned that when artillery and mortar shells exploded in tree tops, the only protection in a slit-trench was to roof one's hole over with logs and earth. And that was the way the Germans chewed up the Belmont Forest into Biffontaine.

The days and nights of the Biffontaine assault left them groggy and shaken, but still there was no rest. Company B, of the 100th, drew a suicidal task. Their order was to rescue the 1st Battalion of the 141st Infantry—a tough Texas outfit—surrounded by Germans east of Biffontaine. The Texans were being literally chewed to pieces by the zeroed in fire from every perimeter.

Price for this job proved a fearful one—as usual. It was a wonder how any man could live through it. But the Texans were liberated. And they came out of their own hell — tearful with gratitude. "God bless you little bastards," they said. "Your faces are the best sight we've seen in this war."

Reward for this bitter fighting in the Vosges was another bivouac—this time at Bain-les-Bains, fifteen miles south of Epinal, once a fashionable spa where the rich and privileged Frenchmen came to drink, rest, and take the water cure. Luxury of this rest, for those who had survived the Vosge, lasted only three days.

For now the 100th was attached to the 44th Antiaircraft Brigade, and were trucked to Nice — to relieve an airborne unit patrolling the Franco-Italian border. Their new front was a twelve mile slice of snowy mountains between Etuenne de Tines and Martin de Vesubie. It was a new experience in this mad and incomprehensible war, for AJAs to emerge as Alpine troops.

But the assignment turned out to be favorable mountaineering, compared to what they had known in the past. Officers and men were all issued parkas and winter gear, and billeted in the sudden

[6]*Ibid.*, p. 227.

luxury of the area's tiny resort hotels and private homes. Their patrol was in a winter wonderland of snow and pine forests. The mountain billet was good for the AJAs. At the dances in the little hotels, the Japanese boys went assiduously to work teaching the local orchestras to swing it American style, and the rosy-cheeked mountain girls how to step it off the way it was done back in the States. But, like all good things, their mountain assignment was too perfect to last.

Back to Nice, and from there to Menton, to join up again with their 442d. Back to the fighting front again, trucked across the Menton-Sospel road, and the usual infantryman's trudge up the snowy slopes to relieve the First Special Service Battalion from their homey dugouts. The 100th was given the wintry job of patrolling the sector north from Menton to the sector held by the 3d Battalion of the 442d, at Mt. Gramando. In all, the AJAs were custodians of eighteen miles of the roughest kind of terrain.

But it wasn't the toughest kind of fighting. Patrols occasionally caught it from German nests, and were blown to bits by Jerry mines and traps. And always there were the persistent and ever-present snipers. But, after what they had gone through, even this kind of war was tolerable.

As winter faded in their sector, and it became mud instead of snow, it was plain that no decisive battles were to be a part of the Franco-Italian Alps. The big show now was at Ardennes and the Bulge, and the men fed on rumors that there might possibly be a sudden ending to the war.

Then came March of 1945, and in spite of the happy speculation, the war proved far from over for the 442d, and its fighting 100th. Now it was train back to Marseille. At Marseille there was one hopeful sign. The unit was ordered to dump all its weapons at this French port. Buddhaheads and kotonks alike believed that, by this gesture, the war was over for them. Everyone imagined they were going home.

The hope grew even more substantive when the embarkation orders included the stripping of all identifying insignia from the men's uniforms and helmets. Unarmed, unmarked, the entire

442d trudged aboard the waiting LSTs. Their port was secret—but it turned out to be the well known and familiar Leghorn. The men, nursing on hope, were not at all dismayed in the strange way they were returned to Italy. But some of the exuberance began wearing off when they were convoyed by truck to a staging area near Pisa. Smiles turned to grimness and even tears when the entire corps were re-equipped with new weaponry to replace the guns, mortars and vehicles left behind at Marseille. Here at Pisa the combined 442d got a fresh crop of replacements from Shelby, and for three days there was intensive practice with the new armaments, and to acquaint the men from Shelby who were replacing the men left buried in the Vosges, in the sober art of killing and getting killed.

Every AJA knew that, for them at least, the war was on again—and for real. When they were rolled out of Pisa, at least the field officers knew that they were being attached to the 92d, a Negro division, and that all these odd-faced citizens out of America were to be hurled against the Germans, in a surprise attack. Their job was to knock out that impenetrable sector at the extreme flank of the Fifth Army line along the Ligurian coast.

This time, as they jumped off into battle at Piestrasanta, it was truly "go for broke." Georgia Hill was their first objective. And what an objective! German emplacements were everywhere—protected by U-shaped trenches, sixty feet in width, forty-five feet in length, with vast forward approaches sown like a bean field with buried, non-metallic, undetectable Shu mines. Every trail, every approach, was booby-trapped. To send men out into this, was like consigning a human soul to hell.

When casualties began to confirm that this sweat-pot was zeroed in with interlacing gun and mortar fire, the green and frightened 92d panicked. In spite of the drivings of their officers, the men behaved badly. So, once more the brunt of the cruel battle fell on the weary shoulders of the AJAs. Faced with one of the dirtiest, most suicidal tasks yet given to the little men, the platoons moved slowly, and with caution, across the mine fields. The lanes were plotted, but they were exposed and, as expected, the men were soon groaning and dying under the merciless butchery.

With hips slithering through the spring mud, like cautious reptiles, with noses close enough to plow the poisonous and miasmic muck, AJAs, in common with other infantrymen in battle, could only wonder how, and for why, they had gotten themselves into this predicament. Relentless as ants on the prowl, these men crawled as long as they could crawl.

In their thoughts there could not help but be sadness and bitterness. None of the superpatriots who, back in California, had maligned the Japanese, imprisoned their families, and stolen their wealth and substance, were on hand to see the men they so frantically hated, pay out their lives as Americans in these cruel infernos of Italy and France.

"Surely, there *can't* be much more," they despaired in thought. With Germany and Japan both getting their dirty war back upon them—with their Japanese fatherland reeling under the blows— surely there *couldn't* be much more. Everywhere now people were talking that the war was over. But still they died and were replaced, died and were replaced—until so few of the original were left. Always, ever always, there was another dirty job to do.

For the AJAs, fate had decreed, there must be and would be fighting—so long as there was a war left to fight.

CHAPTER TWELVE

FOR half a thousand inductees out of America's concentration camps the war was definitely over. For them, as casualties, it had ended in a crashing finale, a quick death, or a slower, more lingering one. But it was not yet over for others, left behind, or for those still capable of serving. While the victorious Italian campaign had become an urgent and decisive sword into the undergut of Europe, every dying spasm of its struggle was still tied like a nerve cell to the Japanese Americans incarcerated in the crude and sprawling camps.

"My furloughs to Poston seemed like years back," remembers Mr. K. "My little wife had her baby while I plowed Italy's mud with my nose. After lugging two more doses of Jerry's shrapnel into base hospitals, I'd begun wondering whether I'd ever see Poston again. About this time, even that muggy buggy place seemed like heaven to me."

But camp suicides seemed never to be prompted by war's death loss, or among those who had given husbands and sons to the nation's military. Preponderance of those who chose total immolation, or who were rescued in the attempt, seemed to be the Isseis who had openly or covertly resisted the war efforts.

To these people self-destruction was the final and honorable way out. To open one's wrists, and watch the blood of life pulse away—to weakness, insensibility, and then merciful oblivion—was not a particularly difficult way to die. In the camps this form of immolation was not uncommon. Tule Lake surpassed Poston in the number of suicides.

With the advance of fall, letters from Tule were indicative that stress and sorrow were rampant. Perhaps it was the retributive punishment Japan was now taking—the air bombardment, first at Saipan, and now the winter bombing of Japan itself. Perhaps it was General MacArthur's re-entry into the Philippines. Perhaps it was the conviction, even among the camp Isseis, of the inevitability of Japan's utter defeat. A terrible urgency now hung over the recalcitrants; a feeling dark and unanswerable.

New directives out of Washington made clear that a review board had been set up at Tule camp for reconsideration of all its incorrigibles. In the earlier months of the war it had been possible to deport those aliens who asked for it—aboard the ships of neutral nations, such as Sweden's S.S. *Gripsholm*. The problem now was infinitely more complicated. But those still definitely pro-Japan were even yet promised deportation at first opportunity.

But those Niseis and Kibeis having second thoughts about their willful forfeiture of citizenship, and even those Issei aliens who might prefer living in the United States, were to be given one more chance. In both instances, final action on the decision would be deferred until hostilities ceased.

For in many an alienated family there had come storms of doubt. To the camp managers, and the WRA as a whole, it all seemed complicated and a little unreal. The core of the problem lay usually in *papa-san*, the head of the house. To reject the decision of a male parent in this grave matter, or any other family course of action, constituted, in *nihonjin* thinking, a rejection of him. Even though *papa-san* might be guilty of second thoughts, to back down on an issue already decided, to impugn one's rationality or motives, would be to irreparably forfeit both *gimu* and *giri*. There *had* to be a logical way out. That way could be suicide, a sign-in for deportation, or collapse into surrender's inevitable humiliation. At Tule, and to a lesser degree at Poston and the more liberal camps, there was evidence of all three.

It took the bitter experience of war and concentration camps to fill many an American-born Japanese with loathing for the strange and unbending *mores* which tradition had so long settled upon their people. Many of them had developed genuine hatred for *bushido,* and the complex necessities tied to *gimu* and *giri.* Many a Nisei, in face of parental disgrace, had already broken with tradition. They hated the damnable evacuation, its erasure of joy, the travesty on citizenship, the destruction of family. They hated the evil and hideous war, which had set the world aflame, and taken the lives of so many brothers, sons, and fathers. They loathed Japan with irrational ferocity, for having started the slaughter. They thought back to those prewar days of normalcy. In those times there had been no vision of frustration and death.

And with the swift movement of events at Poston, and the drastic decisions now being made for its future, they were no longer sure of anything. Now at last, every internee was face to face with the new and paralyzing decree of the camp's abandonment.

The directives from the War Relocation Authority were clearly stated and categorical. All relocation centers, with the exception of the maximum security camp at Tule Lake, were to be immediately liquidated. Dillon Myer was sympathetic. He openly acknowledged the problems. But what encouragement was inherent in the fact that government at last recognized its gigantic blunder, was being nullified by its new and equally gigantic ineptitude in handling this fresh crisis of dispersal.

Week after week the official pronouncements were published which granted blanket permission to the internees to leave Poston freely and without duress. The great prison camps were suddenly now as easy to enter and leave as the Los Angeles plaza. This, in itself, was a startling switch in attitude. But basically ignored was the paramount question every internee was asking: "Where the hell *are* we to go?"

On block bulletin boards the community analysts and sociologists posted cautionary pieces in the vague hope of forestalling the surprise and bitterness inevitably ahead when the internees attempted to reclaim their Pacific Coast possessions. Others appeared in the *Poston Chronicle*. All of it made dismal and unhappy reading.

Internees needed no official reminders. They knew they were trapped, with no place to go. Fish Harbor had been erased as a security measure. Japanese agriculture had passed to other hands. The thousands of little businesses, from restaurants to flower shops, were being run by patrons with more suitable faces, or had long since vanished as casualties in the grind of war.

In three years of internment and humiliation, not one act of sabotage had been traced to the doors of this people. Their men, once given the chance, had more than creditably borne their share of the war. They had stood respectfully above slander, morbid accusation, and the more normal suspicions directed against them because they had the misfortune to look exactly like the enemy.

But now, at last, America truly knew who its enemy was.

Now they were to go home. But for the vast majority there could be no going home. The JACL continuously warned the internees that they were facing a time of pioneering, fully as difficult and discouraging as the one faced by their fathers. The gentle advice was not to return with belligerence or with arrogance. They were to take humbly, and with patience, whatever they could get. They must constantly trust in the democratic process. They must hold ever and always to the belief that, when this tragic struggle was finally ended, the just claims for their losses would be granted the consideration they deserved.

There was little doubt in the minds of some Poston residents that those evacuees returning to California were in for rude awakening. There was no question about the sensibility and adaptability of their people. The frightening thing was that not even the unmatched patriotism of the Japanese Americans was sufficient to offset the avarice of those who had profited at their expense, or the militance of the opposition arrayed against them.

One had only to read the fresh alarms out of the newspapers and radio to realize that resettlement was apt to be as hard and harsh as the evacuation. California once more was aroused, and that state's antipathy toward return of its "Japs" was blatant and vicious. The Native Daughters of the Golden West had already sped their resolution to the State and Federal governments. "Immediate exchange of people of Japanese ancestry in this country for American prisoners of war held by Japan," it demanded. "No return of evacuees to the Pacific Coast area."[1] The Native Sons, not to be outdone, had now mounted their statewide drive against any coming home; that it "would endanger national security."[2] At their May meeting, in San Jose, they unanimously adopted a three-part resolution: (1) asking Congress to remove citizenship and deport disloyal Japanese-Americans; (2) demanding relocation centers be continued; (3) supporting the proposed constitutional amendment abolishing the citizenship of persons born in this country of alien parents. So far the agitation for such far-out discrimination by national law was confined to California, but the implication was open and obvious. Should such a thing happen, Niseis and Kibeis would be deprived of citizenship, and instantly, by fiat, dropped to alien status. In the Native Sons' resolution there was no clarification as to classification they had reserved for those Niseis who lay buried in hero's graves in Italy.

For months the citizenry of California had been well supplied with stickers for walls and car bumpers reading "NO JAPS IN CALIFORNIA." Patriotic societies seemed to have ample funds in their war chests to underwrite the costs not only of public blasts, but for public and private lobbying.

And the same sort of ferment was at work in other groups. Patriotic females of the California Federation of Women's Clubs, Los Angeles District, had sponsored their own resolution barring AJAs from the coast, and urging repatriation of all "disloyal" Japanese and Japanese Americans. Congressmen from California, Oregon and Washington, urged by superpatriotic constituents, were speaking out against return to their states of the people

[1]See San Francisco *News,* March 9, 1944.
[2]*Ibid.,* March 27, 1944.

they had expelled. Washington's Congressman Warren G. Magnuson had declared, in a public meeting in Spokane, that there were not fifty Japanese among the evacuees who were loyal to this country.[3]

But the camps had been ordered closed. The War Relocation Authority had been directed by Supreme Court ruling, to liquidate. Against a solid and vociferous front of resistance, the internees must now, somehow, find their way home. By bus, and train out of Parker, brave and hardy souls daily took their leave of Poston, to again find lives for themselves in the American mainstream. By the end of May 1944, 22,000 Japanese Americans had left the ten great camps. But the resettlement absorption was making little progress in the state of California. California's news kept careful score on the other states receiving their ex-citizens. Illinois had absorbed 5,000, Colorado 2,500, Utah 1,700, Ohio 1,700. Nearly every state in the Union, except California, had caught this egress in some quantity.[4]

But "back to California" had become the obsession of the internees at Poston, and the greater majority in every other camp. California *was* home, and there could be no other place. On one hand was the government pressure to empty Poston, and the other camps, as speedily as possible. With the same urgency that they had been herded into these vast prisons, and stripped of their every possession, were these inmates now being turned back out into an hostile world. And that world, for most, just had to be California.

Day by day they bled out of Poston, back to the Imperial Valley, the San Joaquin Valley, the rich California coastal plains of their former husbandry. Frantically, fearfully, they returned to try to reclaim the little farms, vegetable patches, and flower horticulture, of which they once were so masterfully adept. But three years of war and avarice had made a difference. The new owners were not about to surrender their prizes gracefully or willingly. Seemingly, the only friends Japanese Americans had

[3]Seattle *Post-Intelligencer*, September 21, 1943.
[4]Oakland, California *Tribune*, May 28, 1944.

in their second crisis was the Japanese American Citizens League, and such fair-minded government officials as Dillon Myer of the War Relocation Authority, John Collier of the Indian Service, and Harold Ickes of the Department of Interior. The Japanese businessmen, returning to Los Angeles, San Francisco, Sacramento, faced an even more hopeless situation. Their little shops, restaurants, grocery stores and flower establishments were totally gone. Those that had survived the exigencies of war were in hostile white hands; the others had disappeared without a trace.

Little Tokyo, in Los Angeles, once a happy, prosperous communal center, was now ethnically Negro and Mexican. It would take years and many a discouragement, before it would flower again as Japanese.

The once mighty Japanese fishing fleet, out of Terminal Island, had ceased to exist. If Fish Harbor ever again were populated, it would never know the genial faces of the Japanese who had been given that unforgettable forty-eight-hour roust.

The returns to California farms, because the land was tangible, and ownership undeniable, became the most noticeable, and therefore the most turbulent and violent. The Army had been on hand to drive Japanese off their farms, but it was noticeably absent when it came to reinstating the rightful owners to their properties. In many localities, waves of terror, aimed at intimidating and discouraging returnees, was instituted, and with considerable success. Those who showed the courage to claim their homes and farms, were shot at, brutally beaten, and subjected to burnings and constant threat.

The American Legion, at its convention held in San Francisco, spoke eloquently out against the Japanese blight. With the eyes of a seer, and with voice of thunder, its Department Commander, Leon Happell, trumpeted: "We must look at this problem as of 100 years from now, when 150,000 Japanese will have multiplied and multiplied. This is not the time to take the Japanese out of the camps . . . !"[5]

[5] *The Daily Californian*, August 19, 1943.

But the government had decided it *was* the time. To 110,000 Japanese Americans it proved a turbulent and unforgettable experience.

After twenty-four incidents of arson and violence had been reported against returning Japanese — twenty-two of them in California alone—the Attorney General of the United States gave official warning to local sheriffs to protect the Japanese Americans in their just rights, or face accountability.[6] This was difficult, when even such liberal newspapers as the Los Angeles *Daily News* was attacking the return of the Japanese, under the very name of its publisher, Manchester Boddy.[7]

It was not to be expected that the Hearst papers, who had battled the "yellow peril" for decades before Pearl Harbor, would editorially welcome back the Japanese they had so consistently resisted down to the day of their expulsion. On May 20, 1944, the Los Angeles *Examiner* had gleefully announced that Post No. 1614, Veterans of Foreign Wars, had garnered 200,000 signatures for an initiative petition to amend California's Alien Property Act so that "those persons ineligible to citizenship under U. S. naturalization laws . . . could not acquire, lease or transfer real property or water craft."

The Grange Masters, representing 125,000 agricultural members from the five western states, at their meeting in Portland, Oregon, had adopted a resolution demanding that the federal government "prevent persons of Japanese extraction from returning to the West Coast after the war." Unitedly it condemned the WRA for conducting a "propaganda campaign" to make resettlement of Japanese palatable to patriotic Americans in the farm belts.[8]

Amid this climate of hysterical resistance, it seemed quite proper that the American Legion Post, at Hood River, Oregon, on December 14, 1944, should erase from their county war mem-

[6]*New York Times*, May 18, 1945.
[7]See Los Angeles *Daily News*, issue of May 19, 1944 and *passim*.
[8]New York *Herald-Tribune*, August 22, 1944.

orial the names of sixteen Americans of Japanese ancestry, at the very moment serving their country on the European battlefield.

Many agriculturists—facing the return of their impoverished former neighbors with plaintive demands for the properties and implements they once had owned—had grown increasingly impatient about waiting for the government to act for permanent exclusion. This irritation was further increased when the "yellow-bellies" showed JACL inventory lists of properties and implements forcefully abandoned years before, and abetted by official-looking documents issued by the WRA. Fired by patriotic groups, and the almost universal bleating of the newspapers, many local citizens took matters into their own hands.

Newcastle, California, was only one of the many hot spots. The former neighbors of Summio Doi didn't want him back on the farm he had been forced to leave. Other tenants had harvested good crops on it while he had chafed and fretted out the years at Poston. But in spite of warnings, Summio Doi and his family moved back into their little house. The neighbors promptly set dynamite to Summio's ranch buildings. Miraculously the harassed AJA discovered the explosives in time to extinguish the fuses on the charges that would have destroyed everything he owned.

Summio made desperate appeal to the local sheriff, but to no avail. What he imagined was a caravan of welcoming neighbors turned out to be something else when the neighbors proceeded to shoot up his house. The next night he again found dynamite under his buildings. This second attempt thwarted, they managed to set fire to one of the ranch structures. But Summio Doi — made of the same substance as the kotonks at Belvedere and Biffontaine—hung grimly and desperately on to his birthright as a citizen.

Then there was the case of Minoru Ohashi, at Madera, California — the little city that proclaimed itself as gateway to Yosemite. To Ohashi, it was more like a gateway to hell, when it came to reclaiming his ranch in the fertile San Joaquin Valley. Like so many others, the angry neighbors of this returned evacuee had armed themselves. Acting in concert as a mob, they fired five shots into Ohashi's home. Corporal Y. A. Kawamoto, on leave from the United States Army, and visiting his brother-in-law Minoru, narrowly escaped being killed by the lethal ambush. Threats, night riders, burnings, beatings, were the lot of the gutty little evacuees who returned to the acres they legally owned. With the great camps closing behind them, with expulsion in reverse, they had no other choice but to return home. They found their property stripped, and their holdings appropriated by their neighbors. There was little redress in the courts. Years later, a guilt-ridden nation would attempt some expiation for its crime against a people. Settlement would eventually amount to perhaps ten cents on the dollar of loss. But right now an evacuee was lucky to preserve his life. To start again took a desperate sort of courage. To go home was anything but an happy thing.

For a public figure to go against the grain of an aroused populace took its own measure of courage — for even California's attorney general, and later its war governor, Earl Warren, had testified before the Tolan Committee of Investigation:

"I want to say that the concensus of opinion among the law-enforcement officers of this State is that there is more potential danger among the group of Japanese who are born in this country than from the alien Japanese who were born in Japan.[9]

But there *were* Americans in high office who were aroused to indignation by the shabby treatment continuously accorded the AJA from the time of the war's inception.

One stalwart hero to this people was Harold Ickes, Secretary of the Department of Interior. From Washington, Ickes denounced the growing hoodlumism, by reminding Americans in general, and California in particular, that Nisei sons and brothers of the harassed evacuees were still bravely facing the enemy in the warfronts of the world. That what they were doing was far more in the tradition of Americanism than was the private ven-

[9]See Alan R. Bosworth, *America's Concentration Camps*, p. 73.

detta being conducted safely at home by the racists of the Pacific Coast and elsewhere. In his syndicated news column, Ickes cried out against this violence and discrimination. Finally, at the risk of being publicly branded a Jap-lover, Ickes went to California, and verbally castigated those who were making a farce of the democratic tradition.

Publicly he blasted Governor Bucker, Governor Edge, Mayor LaGuardia, and the vacillating stance of Governor Warren of California. At the San Francisco Commonwealth Club, on April 14, the "old carmudgeon" cried out against self-righteous bigots whe were clubbing, shooting and terrorizing those evacuees trying to return home. As could be expected, it raised a storm of protest from the superpatriots who could see nothing good in a "Jap."

An example of the answer was contained in a D. A. Stowe editorial in the Los Angeles *Herald-Express*. Ickes was reminded that the Japanese had had "covetous eyes" on the Pacific Coast for a long time. "Why give them a place at all in this fair land of ours?" he was asked. "No, Mr. Ickes, we have not missed the Japs. We do not need them. Ninety-five percent of the people on the Pacific Coast āre unalterably opposed to their return here under any conditions. . . . Some say under the Bill of Rights and civil liberties they are entitled to the same rights as civilized people. Very well, then, let's scrap those bills."[10]

Between the public utterances of such men as Harold Ickes, the militant fight of the American Civil Liberties Union, the quiet and determined efforts of the JACL, and the more dedicated members of the WRA, the going home went slowly and painfully on.

Those internees who had elected to go east were faring better, although the Governor of Arkansas had signed a bill preventing Japanese from owning land in the state.[11] And even as far away as Delaware and New Jersey, they were meeting resistance and troubles. "If they are safe and loyal," queried the eastern press, "why not return them to their farms in California?" Here, as

[10]Los Angeles *Herald-Express*, May 26, 1944.
[11]Feb. 16, 1943. Box No. 6, Poston Collection, University of Arizona Library.

in California, local farmers were holding mass meetings and violent protest. Even in Brooklyn, New York, the police were called to forestall public riots against a downtown hostel conducted for the benefit of homeless AJAs.[12] Terrorized wives and widows of service men clung on to the changed world of Poston. There was not much else they could do. They had no men on hand to fend for them in the hostile jungle outside. So long as the big triheaded camp functioned, they, and hundreds of homeless families would hang on to the only life they knew.

The camp's little newspaper now was forced to chronicle the roughings that the returning evacuees were receiving at the hands of their former neighbors. In columns alongside were recorded the happier experiences of those families in the "softer" areas of California, Oregon and Washington, where returnees had found it less strenuous and easier. These were hectic days for the *Chronicle,* cut back as it was in circulation and issuance. Poston's magazine had, long ago, become a complete and final casualty. So the *Chronicle,* as best it could, and as long as possible, struggled to hold the mirror up to its readership in the three slowly deflating camps.

With summer came the *Obon* or *Bon* observance that required coverage. The function was part of the Japanese Buddhist tradition. Special services were held at the Buddhist centers, in the recreation halls, and more particularly in the many homes where death had visited.

When *Bon* came, the bereaved families made special offerings before the ancestral death tablets on their own family *butsuden.* Where death had struck this past year, neighbors and friends called to commiserate tearfully. Then, with mourning over, the mood changed. On Saturday night, Poston's orchestras tuned up for the *Bon* dances. Now, in a switch to gayety, the spirits were dismissed, and, unminded and unheeded, they retreated from their former haunts—until the *Bon* of another year. Poston

[12]*Ibid.,* Box No. 7. April 12, 1944; April 29, 1944.

laughed her way out of sorrow. At the dances, in the *nihonjin* way, the people grew happy again.

At the previous fall's *Higan*, on September 23, another Buddhist holiday had been observed—the people's way of marking the autumnal equinox. Shintos of Poston celebrated it also under the name of *Shunki Korei Sai.*

On November 3 had come the *Meiji Setsu*, and not even a war with the mother country had put complete quietus on this observance by the Isseis to the memory of Emperor Meiji the Great. In a concentration camp, of course, there could be only private readings of Meiji's Rescript.

Shogatsu, or New Year's, had gone big in Poston, just as once it had in Fish Harbor, Little Tokyo, or any other Japanese community. There had been a dearth of the traditional *sake* for the three-day holiday, but the boys running the trucks between Parker and Poston had smuggled enough American booze to make up for this lack—and Poston's *tofu* factory had worked overtime to manufacture a sufficiency of cakes.

There had been the New Year's offerings and prayers before the Buddhist and Shinto shrines. Debts, as always, had been meticulously acknowledged and, wherever possible, paid. The priests had visited the bunkhouses, and had purified them with prayer. On their little stoves the internees had made the traditional *mochi*, or rice dumplings. Those women whose men were dead or absent shared the food, and a bottle or two of wine together, and wept and mourned over the absent men in their lives. Afterwards they had invited their friends in for the *mochi*, and the happier moments.

There had been the *Hina Matsuri*, or Girl Day and Doll Festival, on March 3. Since it was a family holiday, honoring the girl children, especially those born during the year, there had been hundreds of parties in the three camps. There was the traditional gift of dolls, and the gathering of these hundreds of touching little reminders in special alcove displays in the recreation halls.

On May 5 had come its counterpart, or Boy Day—the *Tango No Sekku,* or *Koi Nobori.* At this special time, all the families who could boast of boys, hung their colored banners and the huge red paper carp from the poles outside the bunkhouses.

There were many more native holidays; some of them intimately connected with emperor worship, and, at Poston, privy only to the observance of those who were unregenerate Isseis. American observances were far more open and noisy. Every national holiday, from Christmas to Independence Day, had been enthusiastically observed in Poston. Every bond drive, every Red Cross rally, every blood campaign, had been unstintingly supported. And even as the population waned, and slowly melted away, the internees lived and talked as Americans. Niseis especially, held high their privilege of citizenship. And most internees clung to the faith that this great democracy—providing they believed, and had patience—would eventually right the wrongs.

As spring had advanced, one sensed an epoch was ending, and another one already was settling itself for a share of life and living. Never was the war more bitter or more curious—notwithstanding the sense of victory that was in the air. Already, for the dead, the mighty struggle was over—but for the living, no longer was there a gnawing fear of defeat.

After collapse of the Italian campaign, the great Allied push was on in the Ruhr. Planes by the thousands were pouring their missiles of death upon Nazi and Japanese alike. The conflict had reached such point of fury that all the steel and explosives in the world could not long sustain it.

On April 12, President Franklin D. Roosevelt died under strain of the conflict, and there was weeping among those internees who remained at Poston. Two weeks later Mussolini was hanged by his own people in Milan square, and two days after that came vague reports that Hitler had committed suicide.

After that, events moved overwhelmingly fast. The great German war machine suddenly crumpled into abject surrender. On May 8, the new American President, Harry Truman, formally announced V-E Day, and the final end of the war in Europe. What was left of Poston cheered itself hoarse.

The huge camps which, under Japanese compulsion, industry, and love of beauty, had been brightened with gay colors, rock gardens, tiny lawns, and a profusion of shrubs and flowers, now looked sad, withered and neglected. As the busses had hauled away their daily toll of friends and neighbors, bravely trying again for foothold in hostile America, Poston had become more and more an haunting shell.

Disastrous fires had wiped out some of the flimsy buildings, including the tofu cake factory. These lay in their ashes, never to be rebuilt. The *Chronicle* had whispered itself out, and died. The *Bon* observance had been about the last thing it recorded. Given another year or so, all of Poston, with the exception of the permanent adobe buildings at administration center, would by fire, theft, and elemental dissolution, be reduced again to desert. Given a decade, passing travelers would have neither knowledge or visual evidence of the fantastic drama of waste and futility once acted out to finish in Parker Valley.

The huge warehouses, once stuffed to fatness with the subsistence necessities to one of Arizona's largest cities, were empty, and their wide doors flapped and creaked in the wind. With dwindling population, and the phasing out of WRA, the familiar faces, office personnel, and the corps of stress experts, all had gone into new worlds of endeavor. One warehouse and a few trucks were enough to keep up with Poston's present needs.

As in the days of Fish Harbor, Poston's last haunting population was now again predominantly women and children. They continued their swims in the canal basins. Fellow swimmers were scarce, and the rocked and landscaped approaches to the basins, pretty and promising a year ago, had already gone the way of the dying camps. With lack of attendance and use, rattlesnakes once more were found around the margins of the wide pools. It was not at all like the gleeful experiences of other times. The familiar, friendly, happy faces were gone—never to return. The once noisy hordes of school children had shrunk to a few youngsters, themselves quieted by the solitude, and saddened by the worries of their parents.

Many Army wives were holding out for the return of their husbands from service. Even the WRA was unable to answer the problem of its lonely female internees. Under the pall of uncertainty, the wait was no happy one.

It was difficult for Poston's Service wives and mothers not to be furious about the resistive antics of the American populace, and the irresponsible attitude of certain politicians, veterans' organizations, and patriotic societies. Having been so long away, and having suffered so desperately under the heel of oppression, one could easily believe that all Americans were like that. What was even more appalling was that the government, by legislating into law the right to imprison segments of its own citizenry in times of war or calamitous fright, had set an unjust and dangerous precedence that would last until some future generation could courageously strike this unwarranted privilege from the books.

But such speculation was comfortless in this hour. To its remaining tenants, Poston was now a haunted place. It sat framed through a strange, mad summer. The returning heat burned in upon structure and man. It baked the earth of the Arizona desert, withered the pathetic greenery, once nurtured by its toilers, to the rust and drab of the world beyond the gates, and turned the acres of its flimsy buildings into ovened pie-shells of emptiness. The ghosts walked, and in ghost talk their eerie words came in a thousand memories.

Instead of the gleeful squeals of children, the roar and shouts at the baseball diamond, the chatter and gossip of a city under pine and tarpaper, there now was only the clang, batter and moan of the oven-hot wind in the now vacant shells of the living. Once more the swirl of dust rolled like a fiery breath across this strange and unnatural world of man.

To these last internees it was more than a seared and sagged inferno of haunts. These final reluctant and fearful souls rattled around in the camps. The big place, with few people, was a hollow mockery to reason and purpose.

On one hand was the pressure of the WRA toward getting their remaining renitent and laggard charges out of the camps and back into America's mainstream of living. On the other hand these holdouts faced the deterrents occasioned by their absent men, the utter inability, no matter how hard they tried, to find housing and jobs outside. And they were panicked and paralyzed by the tales of atrocities and terror seeping back to camp from those braving the hostility of superpatriots and agitators in every area where they were attempting a going home. And the memories that haunted, plagued, and heaped up their sadness! Who could forget the hot bus trip from Santa Anita? The arrival in the night? How long must one live before there was a forgetting of the stuffing of straw into mattress bags; the half finshed barracks; the bad food; the way the desert fought back? There was no switching off the memory of family separation because of "integrity," or of death in the desert.

How could one forget the bonfires, the shouts, the turmoil of the great uprising? The pause for mediation? What of the schools, the churches, the holidays, the socials, the births, the deaths, the triumphs, the defeats? Poston was not yet as dead as some of those it had killed, but it was haunted like a graveyard with the shades of memory.

For closer companionship in the ghoulish and unnatural world about them, the remaining internees moved into the barracks nearest the administration center of Poston I, and those mess halls the WRA was still able to keep open for the dwindling population. What they hauled to the new quarters in the dying camp, represented in total what they could likely ever claim in worldly goods.

As event piled on event this strange summer, it was apparent to everyone that the war was about finished. The awful struggle was heading for its last deadly climax. MacArthur was trumpeting the reconquest of the Philippines. But this final victory had cost America sixty thousand lives.

ALL THAT IS LEFT OF POSTON RELOCATION CAMP

The permanent adobe buildings of the administration center are all that remain of the City in the Sun. The U.S. Government retains the buildings for a Job Corps training center. The acres of pine and tarpaper barracks have long

Death now rained on Japan from the skies. War had come at last to her shores with a ferocity her jingoists could never have envisioned on that long ago day at Pearl Harbor. In August came the bomb that obliterated Hiroshima in one searing blast. And three days later Nagasaki was melted and vaporized. The end came quicker than anyone had anticipated or expected. While Nagasaki and Hiroshima smoldered in white ashes and poison smoke, Japan surrendered. The emperor humbled himself before the world. The war in the Pacific came to halt with the same suddenness with which it had commenced.

* * * *

"I got off the train at Phoenix, bought an old Buick off a used car lot, and talked the Phoenix rationing board out of enough gasoline stamps to assure one family's journey from Arizona back to California," Mr. K. thoughtfully remembers. "When I went back through Poston's unguarded gate, it was like chugging into a ghost town. I couldn't believe my eyes. When I held my wife once more in my arms, and stared at my tiny boy for the first time, I had no sympathy or use for the dead camp. We got the hell out—and quick.

"It didn't take that old Buick long to grind us forever out of the Colorado River Relocation Center—and north toward Parker. This time we went home—by way of Needles and Barstow."

One can believe that these expatriates, like most Poston tenants returning to California to fight for a new start, paused, or stopped a minute, to gaze on the huge spread of camp to which their lives for three long years had so inextricably been tied.

The water tower, Poston's only important landmark, still stood, pointing skyward in the desert like a soiled finger. Endlessly its rows of tarpapered barracks shimmered and baked in the still hot sun of early fall. This was Poston I. But they were leaving it at last.

The shrubs, trees, flowers and tiny lawns, which even yet softened the camp's ugly face, had come out of the tireless and compulsive urge of Japanese people to beautify and put in order

213]

their immediate world of contact. Outside the big gate, no longer patrolled, spread the acres of fields so recently tended by the camp's farmers. All this — buildings, lumber, fence, shrubs, fields—now destined to enhance the wealth of the Colorado River Indians, sharp-witted and bargain-hunting Anglos, or to sink back into the gray desert.

Like other Japanese Americans, they were convinced that the camps had been a tragic mistake. But, no matter where or how, no one lived for nothing. At least they had learned what it was like to be adaptable and useful. They *had* tried to make the best of a bad situation. There hadn't been many cry-babies in Poston.

It was the last good look. In that moment there should have been soft music and violins. For, in a few years there would be nothing left of the Colorado River Relocation Camp, known as Poston. And few people driving along this lonely road would ever believe that here indeed was once a city in the sun.

These former internees were probably very thoughtful—and maybe a little frightened—as they headed north for Parker, and back across the Colorado River to California.

A SELECTIVE BIBLIOGRAPHY

Benedict, Ruth. *The Chrysanthemum and the Sword* (Patterns of Japanese Culture). Boston: The Riverside Press, 1946.

Bloom, Leonard, and Riemer, Ruth. *Removal and Return*. Berkeley: University of California Press, 1949.

Bosworth, Alan R. *America's Concentration Camps*. New York: W. W. Norton Co., Inc., 1967.

Edmiston, James. *Home Again*. New York: Doubleday & Company, Inc., 1955.

Feis, Herbert. *The Road to Pearl Harbor*. Princeton: Princeton University Press, 1950.

Grodzins, Morton. *Americans Betrayed*. Chicago: University of Chicago Press, 1949.

Lehman, Anthony L. *Birthright of Barbed Wire*. The Santa Anita Assembly Center for the Japanese. Los Angeles: Westernlore Press, Publishers, 1970.

Leighton, Alexander H. *The Governing of Men*. A study of the internees at Poston under stress. New York: Octagon Books, Inc., 1964.

McWilliams, Carey. *Prejudice; Japanese Americans: Symbol of Racial Intolerance*. Boston: Little, Brown & Co., 1944.

Murphy, Thomas D. *Ambassadors In Arms*. The Story of Hawaii's 100th Battalion. Honolulu: University of Hawaii Press, 1955.

Myer, Dillon S. *Uprooted Americans*. Tucson: University of Arizona Press, 1971.

O'Brien, Robert W. *The College Nisei*. Palo Alto: Pacific Books, 1949.

Shirey, Orville C. *Americans: The Story of the 442d Combat Team.* Washington: Infantry Journal Press, 1946.
Smith, Bradford. *Americans From Japan.* Philadelphia: J. P. Lippincott Co., 1948.
Sone, Monica. *Nisei Daughter.* Boston: Little, Brown & Co., 1953.
Sakai, Saburo. *Samurai!* New York: E. P. Dutton & Co., 1957.
Spicer, Edward H.; Hansen, Asael T.; Loumala, Katherine; Opler, Marvin K. *Impounded People.* Tucson: University of Arizona Press, 1969.
Sugimoto, Etsu (Inayaki). *A Daughter of the Samurai.* Rutland: Tuttle & Co., 1966.

PERIODICALS AND NEWSPAPERS

A general listing. See notes for dates and specific citations.

American Mercury.
Bakersfield *Daily Californian.*
Liberty Magazine.
Los Angeles *Daily News.*
Los Angeles *Herald-Express.*
Los Angeles *Times.*
Nation, The.
New Republic.
New York *Herald-Tribune.*
New York *Times.*
Oakland *Tribune.*
Pacific Citizen. Los Angeles: Weekly newspaper published by the Japanese American Citizens League.
Pacemaker, The. Published at Santa Anita Assembly Center for the benefit of the Santa Anita internees.
Poston Press-Bulletin. Published at Colorado River Relocation Center; superseded by the *Poston Chronicle.*
Poston Chronicle. Published at Colorado River Relocation Center for the benefit of that camp's internees.
Poston Notes and Activities. Magazine; 76 pp. and cover; published at Colorado River Relocation Center. Compiled and edited by Henry Mori.
Rafu Shimpo, The. Los Angeles: Japanese language daily newspaper.
Reader's Digest. New York: July 1945 issue.

[216

San Francisco *Call-Bulletin*.
San Francisco *News*.
San Francisco *Examiner*.
Seattle *Post-Intelligencer*.
U.S. War Relocation Authority, at Tucson:
Papers, reports, correspondence, publications and related materials, from the files of Edward H. Spicer, head of the Community Analysis Section, War Relocation Authority, 1942-1946. Boxes 1 to 20. Special Collections Dept., Library, University of Arizona. Noted throughout text as the Poston Collection, or Poston Papers.
U.S. War Relocation Authority. Washington: Government Printing Office, 1943-1946:
Wartime Exile. The Exclusion of the Japanese Americans from the West Coast.
The Evacuated People.
People in Motion; the Post-War Adjustment of the Evacuated Japanese Americans.

INDEX

BOOKS OF THE WEST . . . FROM THE WEST